WHAT OTHERS ARE SAYING

"A must read for anyone in a leadership capacity. My teaser is the P.R.O. leadership insight is a masterful articulation, a frame work to take you to the next level in your career, business and life!"

– CEDRIC CLARK, VP Operations, Sam's Club (Walmart)

"The blueprint to achieving goals and ultimately living happier and more fulfilled lives."

– JEFF ADAMSON, Cofounder, Neo Financial and Cofounder, SkipTheDishes; Five-Time Canadian National Wrestling Champion and Pan-Am Games Medalist

"This playbook provides the framework that every leader needs to solve their most pressing challenges in today's world of disruption and transformation. Tanvir's personal stories, experience, and research make the P.R.O. Business Mindset highly relatable. It's motivating, encouraging, and inspiring."

– ANNA FOLI, Sr. Director, FTI Consulting; Former Captain and Player, Ohio State and French National Volleyball Team

"A must read for those just starting their career or leaders at the top. Tanvir's P.R.O. framework is a playbook that directly takes concepts from sports to leading and winning in business.

In a world of digital disruption and where our minds never stop to rest, his stories and insights remind us of the basics (and not so basics) necessary to making big plays in business and in life."

– KELLY MACPHERSON, Chief Technology and Supply Chain Officer, Union Square Hospitality Group

"The seguays from sports to business were awesome. Sports analogies are commonplace but Tanvir expands on them by invoking personal anecdotes in an entirely relatable fashion, to athlete or non-athlete. The stories are personal recollections, not third-party academic constructs. Tanvir then challenges you to ponder the reflexive exercise questions. Answers to these questions consequently lead to practical implementation within the reader's organization should one chose to do so. I wholeheartedly endorse the P. R. O. concept and the book itself."

– PETER VILKS, Assistant Professor, Strategic Management at DeGroote School of Business, McMaster University

"Tanvir takes core concepts from high performance sport and challenges you to bring them into your work. This book cuts through the noise and gets you back to focusing on the meat. If you want to infuse clarity and a competitive edge, read this book with your team and get after your goals like an elite athlete!"

– JEREMIAH BROWN, Olympic Silver Medalist; Keynote Speaker and Bestselling Author of The 4 Year Olympian

"A refreshing, and methodical approach to leading and adapting in disruption. Tanvir's off-season, regular season, and postseason framework smoothly translates to the board room, and is an absolute must for anyone looking to win in business today."

– FEMI AYANBADEJO MBA, NFL Vet; CEO HealthReel Inc. and NASA Tech Partner

"Tanvir Bhangoo offers a play-by-play for turning passion into high performance. This book provides the framework for all to elevate execution, but should be mandatory reading for anyone transitioning from sports."

– Dr. DREW TAYLOR, CEO and Cofounder, Acorn Biolabs

"A revolutionary business book of our time, giving the unique perspective of success in sports directly translating to success in business through methodologies alike. In a world of digital and technological disruption, we have to be able to react on the fly, which is where preparation, practice and discipline come into play. Tanvir's theories transcend common business practice, while the analogies speak to the competitor in all of us. Do you have the discipline to make your business a success?"

– MATTHEW PRESZ, Retail Sales Manager, Turkstra Lumber

THE P.R.O. BUSINESS MINDSET

How to Lead Amid Disruption and Chaos

BY

TANVIR BHANGOO

Published by TBX Digital Inc. in Canada

Cover design: Elite Authors
Graphics/ Images: Neha Bokhari
Author Photograph: Natalie Roberson

ISBN: 978-1-7779395-0-2 (softcover)
ISBN: 978-1-7779395-1-9 (ePDF)

First Edition

To all leaders in this new disruptive, uncertain world, committed to playing for something bigger than a paycheck.

TABLE OF CONTENTS

Part 2: Game Highlights

FOREWORD

By Jeff Adamson, Cofounder, SkipTheDishes and Cofounder, Neo Financial

I've always been fascinated by the intersection of high-performance athletes, business and leadership. I've been blessed to have experienced this intersection in my own life, first competing for team Canada for over a decade on the world stage and then as an entrepreneur, founding and leading a multibillion-dollar tech company. My professional career, like many, has been full of ups and downs. Fortunately, the thousands of competitions I had as an athlete, prepared me for the challenges that presented themselves.

One of those challenges was when I first met Tanvir. We were working on a large, industry defining opportunity. We both had a seemingly insurmountable amount of work in front of us. Impossible timelines, not enough resources and no one believing that we could make it happen. What I didn't know at the time was that Tanvir's experience in leading winning teams had uniquely prepared him to get the job done. In what I now know is Tanvir's signature style, Tanvir was able to rally the right people, align, focus and drive the project to completion, without using fear or ego.

When I made the transition from sport to business, I was surprised at how little had been written on the practical application of the mindset of sports and how it can be applied to success in business. Rarely has someone looked at what skills, tactics and strategies from sports practically translate into navigating the uncertainty and chaos of the modern business world.

Much has been written on the fundamentals of producing world class athletes. One does not need to look far to find biographies, coaching manuals and courses explaining in high detail how to become a world champion. Similarly in the business literary world, there are thousands upon thousands of books explaining the "3 things you need" in order to build a business empire or create "passive income". Many of these books suffer from extreme survivorship bias and are difficult to translate into practical application to the everyday person. For example, what worked for building Google, may not necessarily work for someone looking to lead a team of junior product managers.

The lessons learned in sports are often incredibly painful and memorable. Whether it's suffering from a heartbreaking loss, recovering from an injury, or rebuilding a team who has lost its best talent, readers will benefit from Tanvir's learnings having been through it firsthand. Myself having also been through this can attest to the accuracy of his learnings. Tanvir explains these in incredibly structured and easy to implement ways that do not brag or show off his own accomplishments. If anything, he focuses on the lessons he has learned through his own shortcomings so that we may not need to experience them ourselves, and can create strategies to avoid them altogether.

Tanvir roots his own definition of performance in the real-life experiences he has had as both a high-performance athlete and as a high achieving professional with relatable stories of exactly how these lessons were learned, so that the reader can see very clearly how the learnings play out in the real world. These stories include his own experience of being on both championship and losing teams, and translating his experience to working with some of the world's largest brands.

I particularly related to the story Tanvir shares about being proud but never satisfied. After winning a game, Tanvir's coach instructs the team to run and do push-ups up and down the field instead of relaxing and recovering for the next game. This drilled into the team that they cannot get comfortable and being "good" is not good enough. The business landscape, especially in recent history, is littered with companies that were good, even great, only to have another, hungrier competitor rise up and steal their market share. This also happens in careers. After closing a deal, solving a difficult problem, or getting a promotion, it's good to acknowledge your success, but you must stay hungry and focused on your long-term goals.

Given my background as an athlete, I acknowledge that I am biased in my opinion that the mindset, skills and strategies from sports are valuable in all aspects of life. I owe much, if not all of who I am today, to what I learned as an athlete and to the people who helped me along the way. The lessons I learned are infused with the euphoria and despair that come from the summits of high achievement and the deep valleys of failure. They are with me morning, day and night. I am happy to see that Tanvir has dedicated himself to sharing the stories and learnings from sports so that people from all walks of life can have a blueprint to achieving their goals and ultimately living happier and more fulfilled lives.

Jeff Adamson

PREFACE

We're all battling uncertainty.

We're all battling change.

We're all battling disruption.

We're working longer hours and doing more than we've ever done.

The world that we live in is disruptive, fast, and, at times, chaotic. Rising consumer demands, technological innovation, competitive pressures, and digital business models continue to force organizations to adapt. If we are to thrive in this new world, we must learn how to lead in a digital world.

By leading in a digital world, I don't mean learning how to code or program. Instead I mean:

- Moving faster and making adjustments more frequently
- Making quick decisions
- Being adaptable and more nimble
- Reducing turnover
- Delivering results in high-pressure environments
- Changing and innovating without fear

- Executing among noise and distractions
- Managing up and across the organization

What are the closest things to leading and winning in uncertain, disruptive, changing environments? Sports teams and elite-level athletes. Every little thing about a sports team—the way it finds talent, runs practice drills, builds and executes a playbook, plans for contingencies, makes adjustments, builds comradery, handles failure, celebrates small wins, and handles adversity—all of it is driven by the fact that they play a sport that is fast, chaotic, and unpredictable. Oftentimes, the difference between first and second place is merely a couple of inches. I believe that sports teams embody all the characteristics needed to thrive in the post-pandemic future.

Both sports and businesses are built by people who want to win and achieve a common goal. And as the years go by, business environments are starting more and more to resemble the environment of a Sunday night game.

With that belief, this book teaches the P.RO. business mindset, a framework to lead and thrive in a disruptive, fast-paced, changing world, built on principles from championship-winning sports teams. However, this book is not just for athletes, sports fans, or weekend warriors. I truly believe anyone, whether they like sports or not, can learn and apply the concepts and boost their personal and organizational performance.

P.R.O. BUSINESS MINDSET HISTORY

As I embarked on my corporate journey after my MBA, I would often ask myself questions such as:

- Why can't we become the best team in the company?
- Why are we not growing faster despite all the hard work?
- Why are people quitting in the middle of a project?
- Why do I need to spend five years in the same role before I can get promoted?
- Why do some people on the team not care? They're spending most of their waking moments at work. So why are they not motivated and driven like my teammates were back in college football?
- Why are some people OK with lack of accountability and missing deadlines?
- Why is there friction between teammates and departments, especially when we're all working toward the same goal?

I was constantly comparing the success of a corporate team to that of a football team. As I started managing teams and overseeing larger transformations, I began noticing patterns on what separated some of the successful initiatives from the unsuccessful ones. I started uncovering why some teams found success while others came up short. Whether it was projects I was leading or watching the leaders I reported to, I started uncovering the genetic makeup of successful initiatives. I discovered that it was the same regardless of the department, company, or industry.

What separated success from failure was not the use of proprietary technology, specialized skills, or highly talented individuals. Instead it came down to having the right teams and foundations, executing consistently, and pivoting and adjusting as needed. When I looked back at what allowed me to deliver on some high-stakes, high-impact projects at global companies, despite tight timelines and lack of resources, it all came down to the people and execution.

Whether it was leading end-to-end digital transformations, building new teams in record times with zero turnover, launching brand-new digital platforms, deploying tech across thousands of locations, improving app store ratings by four times, or finding over seven figures in savings, it all came back to people and execution.

What surprised me the most was the striking similarity between what I had learned from football and how I led and executed in business. So in 2019, I decided to reverse engineer these concepts and build some sort of a measurable, teachable, and repeatable framework.

The result? **The P.R.O. business mindset.** A methodology that is built from principles and concepts leveraged by professional athletes and championship-winning sports teams to make big plays in business. It includes three stages, starting with the end in mind:

P: The **P**ostseason/ **P**layoffs (optimize and gain momentum),
R: The **R**egular season (execute and implement), and
O: The **O**ff-season (build and assess).

The P.R.O. Business Mindset was built from primary research, interviews with former pro athletes turned business leaders, and from my own experiences and observations. It is a playbook that can be used by leaders, individuals, or teams to maximize performance and execution in the face of disruption.

And that is what *The P.R.O. Business Mindset* brings to the business world—the playbook to leading and making big plays amid disruption and chaos.

THE BREAKOUT

This book is split into two parts:

Part 1: The P.R.O. Business Mindset

1. Off-season—five chapters
2. Regular season—five chapters
3. Postseason—five chapters

Each chapter includes:

1. A story
2. A concept
3. An action plan
4. An exercise

Some of these concepts may be relevant, and some may not. Some you may be able to use today, and some you may save for later. But I hope that these principles will become a new set of tools and a way of thinking that you can leverage as you execute in fast-paced, disruptive, changing environments.

Part 2: Industry Interviews / Game Highlights
Over twenty punch-packing interview summaries from "The Sports to Business Podcast" with elite-level athletes turned executives and business leaders. Interview guests range from former pro athletes (NFL, NHL, Olympians, and NCAA) to coaches and have held leadership positions at companies including Walmart, SkipTheDishes, RBI, Gold's Gym, Oracle, and DraftKings, among others.

PART 1

The P.R.O. Business Mindset

INTRODUCTION

The Impact of Leadership

"Look how far you've come."

The impact this sentence had on my life is incomparable.

When I was six years old, my parents decided to move back to India. My sisters and I spent just over five years in Punjab, where I completed grades one to six. In 2001, when we all decided to move back to Canada for good, I had some difficulty adjusting. We moved to Brampton, Ontario, about thirty minutes from Toronto. I felt like I had come back to a culture that had moved on, and I didn't fit in anymore. It was tough making friends. Some of the teachers weren't very helpful. My grades dropped from nineties back in India to sixties, and I was placed in ESL (English as a second language) classes.

I wasn't really good at the major Canadian sports either, and I actually got cut from the flag football team in grade seven. I had hit a growth spurt in 2001 and was bigger and heavier than most other kids my age, so that probably had something to do with it. But that same year, I stumbled upon the Brampton Minor

Football Association through a pamphlet in the mail. I thought football would be a good fit for multiple reasons. I had seen it on television, and it looked fun. Since I was bigger than most, I could use my size to my advantage. I was also more on the chubby side, so this was my opportunity to become a little tougher. And I thought I might even make some friends along the way.

So in the summer of 2002, I convinced my parents to sign me up for the house league team. There was a $500 registration fee, which felt hefty at the time, given that only my dad was working while my mom stayed at home taking care of us. Fortunately they agreed. That was the beginning of my football journey.

At first I struggled. I remember having to run down a hallway for a speed test, and I nearly fell as I had a hard time keeping my weight under me. I had to learn how to get into a three-point stance, and I kept falling forward as my arm wasn't used to holding the weight. I would come home, and I would have blue-and-purple bruises all over my upper body. When it came to conditioning, I could barely run a lap around the field. It was a lot, but I stuck with it.

After the summer season was over, one of the coaches asked me to try out for the Brampton Bulldogs rep program for the fall season. I'm glad I did, as that was the turning point in my life. Midway through that season, right after practice on a cold, rainy fall night, the head coach pulled me aside. He asked me to take a walk down the sidelines. I still remember this as if it was yesterday. I was drenched in rain, and my cleats were covered in mud. With my helmet in one hand and my one-liter water jug in the other, I made my way over to the sidelines, not knowing what to expect. Was I in trouble? Did I do something wrong during practice?

As we started walking down the field, Coach said in a calm, comforting voice, "Do you remember when you started playing? You didn't know much about the game. It was your first time playing defensive lineman. Look how far you've come." My confused look turned into a smile. It was one of the very few times that someone had actually taken the time to praise me.

Then he said, "You've become a great lineman and have a bright future. But I want you to remember one thing: never stop improving!" And he gave me a pat on my shoulder pads.

I said, "Yes, Coach!" And with a big smile, I jogged over to the parking lot to find my mom.

And that is exactly what leadership is about. Empowering and enabling your people to grow. It's about giving someone the tools needed to succeed. It's about casually praising someone's efforts and commitment and leaving a few words of inspiration. And in my story, it was about believing in a kid even when the kid didn't believe in himself.

Coach could've just left practice that day and not gone that extra mile to encourage me. He had no monetary reason for doing so. But this is something that great leaders do: giving with no expectation of getting anything in return. Because of those five minutes, I was able to slowly gain back the confidence I had lost. I was able to keep a positive mindset. I had found something to look forward to every single day. The impact it's had on me as an individual grows every year.

The impact we as leaders, colleagues, friends, and humans have on each other is often overlooked. But even the smallest of gestures and acts of kindness can have a huge impact on someone's life, your team, and your mission.

It's never just about strategy, technology, frameworks, projects, budgets, etc. At the end of the day, it all comes down to leadership.

Oh, by the way, we won the championship that year.

SECTION 1

Off-Season: Assess and Build

P—Postseason
R—Regular season
O—Off-season

CHAPTER 1

Punch Above Your Weight Class

Shift Your Mindset

During my first three years at McMaster University in Hamilton, Ontario, our football team record was as follows:

2008: 4–4—Lost in the first round of conference playoffs
2009: 6–2—Lost in the second round of conference playoffs
2010: 6–2—Lost in the second round of conference playoffs

For some background, Canadian university football has four conferences that host a total of twenty-seven teams. We played in the Ontario University Athletics (OUA) conference. Winners of each conference compete for the national championship, known as the Vanier Cup.

We were improving each year and making incremental progress. These were the rebuilding years to put McMaster back on the map as Canada's top football school, under the leadership of our head coach, Stefan Ptaszek, or Coach P for short. Coach P had taken over the head coaching duties in 2006. At the time, Coach P was in his late thirties and had won a pair of national championships, first as a player and then later as the offensive coordinator with Wilfrid Laurier University.

In 2011, in my fourth year, many expected us to go 7–1 or even 8–0 in our conference with a trip to the OUA conference championships. That's as far as anyone believed we could go. But Coach P saw it differently. He dreamed bigger.

Ahead of our next training camp in August 2011, Coach P made an announcement that took us by surprise. It became a big factor in shaping our identity as a football program for the years to come. Coach P announced that during training camp, the McMaster Marauders would make an eight-hour road trip to Laval University in Quebec and face the reigning national champions, Laval Rouge et Or, in a preseason matchup.

This was completely unexpected. Here's why: every year in training camp in university or pro sports, teams organize an exhibition match with a rival team. Years prior we had competed with other teams from our conference in an exhibition match, but *never* did we travel outside our conference, especially eight hours east on the infamous Highway 401 to play against the reigning champions.

To put this in perspective, Laval was the Canadian football equivalent of Ohio State or Michigan State of NCAA football. Since 2003, Laval had never lost more than one game during any season. This was Laval's record for the three years preceding our trip:

2008: 8–0—Won the national championship
2009: 7–1—Lost in the national semifinal
2010: 9–0—Won the national championship

In contrast, the last time McMaster went to the Vanier Cup was in 1967. As much as we believed that the hard work, dedication, and countless hours of training over the past three years had prepared us to go up against anyone in the nation and put up a decent fight, facing the national champions was still going to be something that none of us had ever experienced before. There were doubts.

So at the end of the first week of training camp, we traveled to Laval. As with any practice, we started with our own respective routines, with us on one side of the field and Laval occupying the far side. Soon after, the head coach from Laval, Glen Constantin, asked everyone to jog it in for a prepractice huddle in the middle of the field. By the way, Glen Constantin is one of the most successful coaches in Canadian university football. As of the year of this book, he has won nine national championships as head coach, the highest in the history of Canadian football. As coach Glen blew the whistle, both teams jogged in and took a knee.

Coach Glen said that every year, Laval invites the team that they believe they will face in the finals. They invite the best team in the country to come and practice with them before the season starts, so that they can prepare against the best. He said, "We invite the team that we believe we will see in the Vanier Cup at the end of the season. And this year it's the McMaster Marauders."

If there was any motivation that we were lacking or any doubts that needed to be removed, this was it. Coming out of that huddle, I felt an energy in our team that I had never felt before. The next day in the preseason game, we went in with guns blazing, full of hype, with a mindset that we could compete with Laval. At halftime we were winning 10–5, and we ended the game 24–10 in Laval's favor. Regardless, we left Laval with a sense of confidence and belief that we did not have coming into Laval. A team that three weeks ago had the mental block of aiming only as far as winning our conference finals was now thinking about the national championship. Our anchor had changed.

Here is what happened that year. We finished the season 7–1. We won our conference championship, the Yates Cup, beating the undefeated Western Mustangs at their home field. We then won the semifinal against Acadia University, who were the Atlantic Conference champions. Then we traveled west to Vancouver to play in the national championship game for just the second time in the school's history. Our opponent was none other than the Laval Rouge et Or. We beat Laval 41–38 in double overtime in front of over twenty-five thousand fans at BC Place Stadium. We accomplished something that had never been done before in the history of McMaster football. We won the 2011 National Championship.

That season embarked us on a twenty-one game record win streak, where in my final year (2012) we went back to the championship game and lost to Laval. In 2014, the Marauders went to the national championship game once again and lost by one point. In 2019, the Marauders won another Yates Cup and made it to the national semifinal game again.

What was so different about the teams in 2011 and beyond versus the years prior? The team learned to punch above its weight class. Once we realized we could compete with Laval, we approached our training, our practice, and our season like a championship team. We only compared ourselves to the best team in the nation, and our standard of performance, effort, and dedication started to match that of a championship team. Things started falling into place. And how did it all start?

It started with the leadership. It started with Coach P. Coach P had won a championship as a player and as a coach. He knew what a championship team looked like. In 2011, he knew his team was a championship-caliber team. But we, as players, needed to believe that this was our year. So Coach P did what he believed would shift our mindset and set our targets at the top of the mountain. He put us in a fight with the best team in the league.

Concept:

Before starting on your journey, you need to remove any self-limiting beliefs and aim high. Punching above your weight class means setting targets that are much higher than what you've achieved in the past. It's about committing yourself to a goal that seems impossible at first. In return, it pushes you to shift your perspective, approach, and mindset to achieving these stretch targets.

Everything else in this book builds off of this concept. Leading in a digital, disruptive world is contingent on you shifting your mindset. It affects how you build your playbook, build your team, and execute on your vision. If you want to make big plays, you need to think big.

Because we're now operating amid digital disruption, uncertainty, and change, many preexisting strategies and playbooks are no longer relevant. Tech start-ups have started disrupting stable industries. The skills and capabilities of the past are becoming commoditized. Whether it's entering new markets and competing against the top dogs that once seemed impossible, or trying to defend against new tech-first entrants that are nimbler and faster, both require unconventional approaches. Both require a roadmap that doesn't yet exist. Meaning to thrive amid chaos and uncertainty, businesses and leaders need to reimagine their strategies and think differently.

When we're up against chaos and change, we tend to focus on what worked for us in the past versus reimagining our future. We fall prey to our biases and develop tunnel vision. Our thinking and solutions become limited. Punching above your weight class instead propels you to rethink and reimagine your future. It is a crucial step to winning the game in which the rules are ever changing.

First, it pushes you to rethink your current strategy. You quickly realize that whatever you're doing today is not enough to reach this massive goal. To reach this new target, you may need to form a new plan, find additional resources, pick up your speed of execution, or completely change your direction. Achieving massive goals sometimes requires you to shake things up—which starts with your overarching strategy.

Second, it promotes outside-the-box thinking. Instead of trying to build a faster horse, you start thinking about building a motor car. When you stretch yourself and get outside your comfort zone, you are forced to find unconventional approaches. For example, if all of a sudden your sales targets for the year doubled, you would have to do something drastically different to meet your goals. Maybe that includes building strategic partnerships or launching a brand-new product line. It could also include renting an office space for six months beside a potential client's office in the effort to win them as a client, which could amount to 50 percent of your sales targets alone.

Lastly, it breeds confidence. When you aim higher and put in the work, you start seeing results. When you see results, it gives you positive feedback that whatever you did is working. This feedback encourages you to continue on the path, building confidence in your abilities. This confidence changes how you carry yourself. Your attitude toward work and life changes. You start eliminating any self-limiting beliefs. And like championship-winning athletes, you start to visualize success before you're successful.

Side Note:

I was leading a digital transformation for a global brand, and we had to lay new technology foundations before we could implement the systems and apps to drive digital sales. The technology upgrade was extensive. It required replacing most of the company's existing retail technology

> systems across hundreds of locations. This entailed new technology integrations, extensive testing, in-location logistics, training, actual implementation, troubleshooting, and support. When we were planning the project timeline, our external partners told us that a project of such caliber usually takes companies over two years to complete. Pressed for time, we had about six months to complete it.
>
> I knew that the biggest culprits behind the extended timelines were a lack of logistical planning and issues during deployment. I also knew that we had the right people in the right roles, and if we focused on the details, we could hit the six-month mark. So I shared with my team that not many had been able to accomplish what we were up against, and that if there was a team that could do it, it was us. Motivated by this challenge, the team found new unconventional solutions, such as surveying the retail locations to address any issues beforehand, pretesting each system, and having twice-a-day stand-ups with all external partners to ensure a fast flow of communication and same-day issue resolution. Two quarters later, we had completed one of the fastest technology upgrades without compromising quality or budget, surprising many. We aimed high, and as a team we found a way to make it happen.

Change is inevitable. What seemed impossible in business twenty years ago is now within reach. Speed of innovation is high, and barriers to entry are the lowest they've ever been. The best leaders and organizations will take a step back and aim high, making change and uncertainty their allies. It all starts by shifting your mindset.

Sports to Business:

The very nature of sports and athletics is to outdo your opponent. Teams and athletes that win championships set high targets and work hard to achieve them. Specifically, championship-caliber teams and athletes do the following:

1. **Aim and reach higher**
   Regardless of how many games they won last year or their rank, elite athletes and teams always aim for the championship. They are always striving to improve and get better every single day. If someone is at the top of their game, they continue to set higher goals.

2. **Take risks and do unconventional things in order to achieve high targets**
   Great players make big plays in big games. They're not afraid of making mistakes. They try and test new approaches in their training on their quest to find the edge that allows them to win.

3. **Dig deep and eliminate any self-limiting beliefs**
   Confidence is key. You'll seldom see an athlete who doesn't believe he or she is the best. That's the mentality

that athletes carry, especially those who, as individuals and as teammates, aim high.

4. **Carry themselves as champions and visualize success**
   How championship teams and athletes prepare, act, and carry themselves off the field is a product of their attitude. Those who punch above their weight class visualize themselves as champions before they ever reach the podium.

In business, we don't have leagues or tiers, and we don't have games where you have to show up every weekend and play against your competition. Instead, the season is always on, and you're constantly playing against the best of the best. Those on the top never stop transforming, and those who are hungry will continue to disrupt markets.

This means great leaders and businesses must do the following:

1. **Constantly set stretch targets**
   They must set targets that may seem daunting, which in turn requires the team to readjust their regular course of operations. This drives innovation and pushes a leader to ask "why" and "how" with regard to their goals.

2. **Find unconventional approaches**
   What worked last year won't work this year. When the

targets are higher, and a leader needs to find exponential growth, then they need to think outside the box. In uncertainty and disruption, those who can rethink their approach to meet consumer demands will continue to disrupt long-standing industries.

3. **Shift their mindsets**
   To achieve these targets, leaders must believe that these goals are attainable. They must believe in themselves and ensure that the teams also believe that these targets are attainable.

4. **Build environments that enable success and inspire confidence**
   Whether it's remote, in person, or a hybrid-work environment, the people, office, surroundings, and overall culture play an important part in achieving large goals. Leaders must invest in creating safe and encouraging spaces for their teams to build confidence and make big plays.

Action Plan:

Whether you're leading a team you know is capable of achieving a lot more, building a new team that has to conquer stretch targets, or want to personally make big plays, it all starts with you—the leader.

Here is how you can punch above your weight class.

Step 1: Aim High

Start by setting goals that are daunting and seem out of reach. It forces you to find ways or means to get results that you otherwise didn't believe were possible.

You'd be surprised at what you can accomplish with the right people, execution, and leadership strategies if everyone is marching in the same direction. You need to simply shift your perspective and aim higher. The execution will come. For now, focus on the end, not the means.

As you pick your high-level stretch targets and align your team, which we'll cover in the upcoming chapters, ask yourself whether these goals make you uncomfortable. If you're optimistic that you can achieve them at your current pace, then these are not stretch targets.

For example, if your sales grew by 50 percent year over year, then a stretch target is not another 50 percent. It should be finding 200 percent growth. If your digital transactions are 10 percent of your total transactions and are currently growing 1 percent year over year, then a stretch target should be growing your total digital transaction mix to 20 percent over the next two years. If you're generally 10 percent over budget, then your stretch target should be finding 5 percent savings the next year. If your team has 50 percent turnover, then a stretch target should be to have zero turnover.

A stretch target should feel unreasonable. You know you've aimed high when you know that the only way to achieve your goals is by changing your current way of operating, or by finding new help, or through new innovation, or through additional resources. It should force you to think bigger by taking you outside your comfort zone.

Step 2: Build Your Confidence

You need to show your team that it can compete with the best. Building confidence comes from repetition and practice and from watching other leaders.

To build confidence through practice, find ways to achieve small wins first. This can be low-hanging fruit that builds positive momentum for your team. Then put your team in position to execute on special projects and find ways to place key members in positions to make big plays. Eventually, confidence will grow as you gain momentum. For both, you need to find opportunities where your team members can practice and feel good about their performance. For example, it can be a five-minute demonstration to the executive board or a small product launch led by the team.

But how do you build confidence when you or your team members can't find the opportunities, have never competed at the elite level before, haven't launched big products before, and haven't stepped into larger roles, entered the markets, or disrupted industries with new innovations?

You learn by watching those in front of you. In sports, during preseason training camp, it's unlikely for a first-year rookie player to make the team. That's because in training camp, there are too many players and not enough reps to go around. The lack of repetition makes it challenging for someone in their first year to make big strides within a span of a few weeks.

However, there are some players who do end up making the team, and at times, even win a starting spot. One of the key drivers behind their success, that I've personally seen, is a rookie player's ability to learn by watching those taking the reps while he or she is on the sidelines. A player can mentally learn by visualizing themselves taking the reps that someone is going through on the field, while studying the situation or their opponent. Eighty percent of the benefits can be derived by mental reps, and this accelerates the learning curve substantially.

Similarly, leaders and teams might not have the opportunities or the luxury of slowing down to analyze, try, learn, and then gain confidence over time. Instead, watch those who have done it well, whether in your organization or in a sister industry. Take mental reps and move with speed. Have your team watch those who you believe to be the best, and they'll soon realize that it's ordinary people making extraordinary plays. Whether you're leading a company or working on solo projects, watch, learn, and execute.

Confidence will come.

Side Note:

One day at work, I noticed that my team's confidence wasn't where it needed to be. The projects my team was working on were positioning our business as a leader in the market. Each team member had made great progress, both on a project and personal level. Yet a few of my team members were finding it hard to see just how impactful their actions were on the overall business.

To help boost their confidence, I brought a whiteboard

to one of our weekly meetings. I wrote down the names of every individual on my team, and beside each name, I jotted down their projects and what they had delivered. Then one by one, I highlighted their personal growth and the financial/foundational impact of each project on the business. I also shared how our results were on par, if not better, than our competitors. This simple exercise immediately lifted their spirits. The next day, I saw a team that was ready to compete against anyone in the world.

Step 3: Readjust Your Approach

Unreasonable results require unconventional methods. What worked for you before will not work now. Do not limit your thinking based on what you've done in the past or readily available solutions. Instead, think from the perspective of unlimited resources. If you had access to people, technology, and capital, how would you achieve this super-high target?

This thinking helps remove the biases and tunnel vision that occur when we limit our thinking to what worked in the past. For example, if you need to double your sales goals year over year, biases and tunnel vision may suggest simply hiring more people. But if you truly take a step back, perhaps a strategic partnership with another company could get you halfway there. Or maybe there is a new product that you can sell for a higher price point with a recurring revenue stream.

Rethink how you've done things and find unconventional approaches.

Step 4: Eliminate Negative Beliefs

Our success is highly dependent on our thoughts, which influence our actions. Setting high targets is the first step in leading in digital, disruptive, chaotic environments. But to follow through with it and find long-term success, you need to replace any negative, self-limiting beliefs with positive ones.

Work on eliminating negative thoughts. If you hang around people who constantly complain, you'll most likely find yourself chiming in. If you're in a room full of people where everyone believes that the timelines for a project are too tight, then sooner or later you'll start believing that too. This doesn't mean you ignore the reality or potential risks. It means to understand where you're headed, know what it will take to get things done, understand that it won't be easy, but then believe in yourself and in your team to get it done.

Visualizing success will also help you address obstacles ahead of time. Many confuse visualization with letting go of any negative thoughts. Instead, visualization allows you to think through all the potential risks and scenarios and plan accordingly. It is an objective walk-through of what may occur and how to best prepare. Visualize yourself punching above your weight class and all the work and readjustments you'll need to make. As you work through the scenarios, you will start to build a mental map on the premise of hard work and execution and not negativity or worry.

Exercise:

- Define what success looks like for your team and organization. Is it being known across the industry? Is it launching an awesome app that has over one million downloads? Or is it doing something that's never been done before?

  ____

  ____

  ____

- Are you setting targets based on past accomplishments, or limitless potential? If you can set goals based on limitless potential, what might they be?

  ____

  ____

  ____

- List what is holding you back from raising your performance to the next level in your career or organization.

  ____

  ____

  ____

- What changes would you need to make to your culture, your team's mindset, and your overall mentality so that you can start setting big targets to punch above your weight class?

  ____

  ____

  ____

CHAPTER 2
Build Your Playbook

Championships are Won in the Off-Season

It was November of 2012, and we were facing the University of Calgary in the national semifinal for the first time in my five years at McMaster. Calgary had one of the most explosive offenses in Canada with multiple schemes and high complexity. On film, they looked fast and dangerous. If we were to win that game, it was going to start with us stopping their run attack.

There was one play in particular that I remember vividly. It was early on in the game. Calgary's offense had the ball, and it was first down. They came out of their huddle and lined up in their regular formation, something we had seen on film. Based on their formation, we received our play call from our defensive coordinator, and we also lined up with our counterattack.

A few seconds after scanning our defense, the Calgary quarterback took a step back and did something that we hadn't seen much of before. He called an audible. Within seconds their entire formation changed. They were going to run a completely different play. Any time a quarterback calls an audible, it's usually because he saw a gap in the defensive formation that he thinks the offense can exploit.

We had never faced Calgary. All of the teams we played against were in the Ontario University Athletic Conference, which ran very different offenses. And not many were advanced enough to call audibles and adjust based on our defensive formation. Calgary was a good team, with new, complex, well-executed plays, that had plowed through defenses on their way to this game. We were now facing a situation for which we only had four days to prepare.

But fortunately, our playbook had a set of rules, checks, and balances for these types of situations. Just as their offense was trying to put us in a vulnerable position, our safety called an audible as well. We moved to a different formation based on the rules from our playbook. It was quick, it was clean, and it was smooth. We knew our new alignment and assignment, and we were ready to fire off the ball.

With the play clock winding down, the Calgary center snapped the ball, and they ran the ball to the short side of the field. And we shut them down.

We held one of the best offenses in the league to just six points in that game. We won 45–6 and went on to compete in the national finals.

This one play summarizes the meticulous planning from our

coaching staff in building our playbook. What we did was a result of years of strategic planning and preparation by our coaches, from head coach, to our defensive coordinator and positional coaches. It was like the different parts they had put together over four years had finally taken the shape of a well-oiled machine. We were able to adjust to complex schemes within a matter of seconds.

The coaches knew what it would take for our defense to play at the national level and put together a roadmap to get us there. This roadmap wasn't based on what we needed four years ago, but where we were headed in the future. It included getting the right players on the team, adding multiple schemes, and baking in adjustments. Equally as important were the rules and principles the entire playbook was built on—it was essentially foolproof. It had an answer for all types of offenses.

No matter what offensive formation we faced, the basic rules of the playbook made it super easy for us to shift and adjust. Instead of thinking, we were attacking.

The importance of building a strategy with the end in mind is something I carried with me into the business world. As I built the digital roadmap for a multinational business, I had to build a playbook for where we wanted the brand to go, not where it was today. The actions we would need to take had to align with the long-term goals. This included replacing legacy technology systems with integrated, cloud-based infrastructure to put the company in a position to react, adjust, and capitalize on whatever the future threw its way. And I knew I would have to put in the work up front before the results started to trickle in.

The play serves as a good reminder that championships are won in the off-season.

Concept:

Before you can start executing, you need to build a strategy and invest in the foundations. You need to build your playbook. There's a quote from Wayne Gretzky—"A good hockey player plays where the puck is. A great hockey player plays where the puck is going to be." This can't be more true in business today.

Building your playbook means:

1. Forming a strategy based on your long-term vision (where you need to go) and
2. Building the foundations for future success.

A playbook forms your strategies, roadmap, and execution methodologies to position yourself, your team, and your organization for long-term results. Your playbook consists of a set of plays (business strategies) that you will run (execute) in an effort to win the game (overarching business goals). A playbook acts as the DNA of your business. A set of nonnegotiable rules and core values that you execute against. This is a prerequisite to getting the results you desire as an individual or as a leader.

No great leader ever jumps into a role and starts executing. They take the time to build their personal playbook and plan for the road ahead. This applies to any scenario in business, whether you are solving a problem, scaling a company, or delivering on a project. For example, working toward a promotion, taking on a new team as a senior leader, working on a multiyear product launch or digital transformation, or preparing your organization to find new revenue streams.

It is important to take some time up front to anticipate changes and study the environment. Before jumping into execution, strong leaders analyze where they're headed, who their competition is, and what resources and help they'll need along the way. Instead of blindly going down the most common path, building a playbook helps leaders build a strategy for where they should be going. Not where they're currently headed.

Building a playbook also involves putting in place the right foundations. There are too many distractions, competing priorities, and constant changes in today's business world. The only way to execute with all these factors being present all the time is to focus on building the foundations that will allow you to thrive in such environments.

Building your foundations includes doing the things behind the scenes that others don't see. For example, getting the right people on the team, fixing underlying issues before building new tech platforms, getting buy-in from key stakeholders, and so forth. Identifying and addressing these foundational elements up front increases the chances of success down the road.

Often I hear friends and colleagues blame their teams or external circumstances for not achieving a certain goal or result. But every single time, I can trace poor performance back to lack of planning and positioning. They simply didn't spend enough time preparing up front. For example, a disastrous presentation is rarely the fault of a hard-nosed board member who asks tough questions; it is rather because the presenter did not anticipate the questions ahead of time. Or if a technology rollout across a thousand stores fails, it is rarely just the fault of the vendor; it might have failed because the project leader did not anticipate the risks and edge cases, and failed to put in place the right measures up front.

Having a well-thought-out playbook enables leaders to do big things and move faster down the road, pivot with ease (section 3), and keep a team motivated and marching toward their goals, despite any obstacles or setbacks. In times of uncertainty, it becomes the core anchor that every action must align to. This chapter discusses how to build your playbook and lay out your foundations; the next three chapters dive deeper into building some of these foundational elements.

Side Note:

Most of my leadership roles were in fast-paced transformational environments. I knew that in order to succeed, I had to deliver quick results. But I also knew that if I just started executing and solving the most pressing issues without a playbook, all by myself, I'd run out of steam within a matter of months. So contrary to my instinct of picking the low-hanging fruit as fast as I could, I invested all my time during my first two to three months in building the foundations. This meant recruiting the right people, getting leadership to buy into my vision, studying and separating the underlying issues from symptoms, and adjusting my personal health and fitness routine to maximize my energy and focus. It was all worth it because the teams, relationships, contingency plans, and systems that I built carried me through the toughest moments down the road.

Digital Transformations and the Importance of Playbooks:

Businesses from different sectors, due to tech commoditization and rising consumer demands, have started entering markets that once seemed far-fetched. We've seen businesses built with speed and agility at their core disrupt markets and push others to adapt and transform to combat these new competitive threats. Digital disruption is a reality across most traditional and long-standing businesses today. As a result, most are undergoing some form of digital transformation.

A digital transformation is when a business invests in, and implements, technology to become competitive in a digital-first world. This is achieved by leveraging technology to find or enhance new revenue streams such as e-commerce and mobile ordering, and by reducing costs on the back end through systems, process automation, and efficiencies.

Unfortunately, more than 70 percent of digital transformations fail. Why? It's not because of technology or talent. It's due to the lack of long-term foundational planning, which leads to poor execution. Spending time up front to build a playbook that accounts for short- and long-term scenarios while investing in the foundations "behind the scenes" significantly increases the chances of success. If you're looking to complete your digital transformation on time, under budget, with a positive ROI (return on investment), then don't just execute. First, build a playbook and invest in the right foundations.

Sports to Business:

In sports, a playbook is more than drawn-up plays on a whiteboard. The entire system, team, training, and everything around it are all products of the playbook. It is the core pillar of a team. Specifically, a football playbook entails the following:

1. **Building the Core Strategy**
   The systems and schemes a team will run during the season. It encompasses a well-thought-out strategy for what the coaching staff believes will act as a competitive advantage. It takes into consideration the players, opponents, and potential adjustments a team may need to make.

2. **Building the Foundations**
   The strategy triggers work that happens during the off-season. These are the things that no one on the outside sees until the season starts. For example, acquiring new players based on the playbook, building and practicing specific plays, and having the right checks and balances for various situations.

From a business standpoint, a playbook includes the following:

1. **Business Strategy**
   A business strategy must take into consideration three things: its competitive advantage, where the customer is going, and its internal operations. Leaders need to spend time studying the environment, economics, internal operations, and external variables before picking a direction and forming any conclusions.

2. **Foundations**
   This is what powers a business strategy. Great playbooks always think in terms of long-term success versus Band-Aid solutions. Long-term success requires spending time up front before starting any major project to outline scope, milestones, and risk mitigation, and to identify key stakeholders, align expectations, anticipate potential roadblocks, and plan contingencies for each. It also includes fixing underlying root causes or lingering issues.

Side Note:

As a young executive, I often got questions on how I managed to 'score the role', sometimes implying that I got lucky. In response, I usually asked them what their top three priorities were for the year. When they could not provide an organized answer, I said, "You see, that's how I scored it. I know exactly what I want, and I prepare like my life depends on it."

Action Plan:

In business, there is no predefined off-season. Most of the planning and coaching happens during the game, given the speed and needs of the business. But no championship team ever goes from game to game. They spend the time preparing and practicing in the off-season in order to make big plays in the playoffs. Similarly, in business, it's important to be disciplined and take some time to build your playbook—it will pay you dividends down the road.

Here is a four-stage process to building your business playbook:

Step 1: Identify Your Goals, Correctly

Take your stretch target from chapter 1, and break it down into quantifiable objectives. It's imperative to understand what your objective is. The more granular and quantifiable you can make it, the better. This will help focus your efforts on the foundations that will provide the best ROI.

Your goals may be to grow sales by 30 percent, get a promotion within the year, take over a new team, or reduce turnover by half. Once you have your goal, then building your playbook becomes an exercise of working backward from that goal. The key is to gain clarity on your goals.

It's also important to target the right objective versus solving for visible symptoms. Considering the example of a retail brand, data may show that total sales from digital channels are lower compared to industry benchmarks and competitors. You may conclude that your e-commerce experience is not the greatest, and therefore it makes sense to invest resources to enhance its core functionality.

However, further analysis may show that first-time online transactions are on par with competitive benchmarks, but repeat transactions are much lower compared to competitors, resulting in lower overall sales. This presents a totally different issue than a poor online experience. In fact, there might be numerous underlying issues, such as late deliveries, poor customer service, poor product quality, or a mere lack of value for buying online.

Therefore, it's important to identify the right root causes that need to be solved. In the example above, one would instead focus one's efforts on perhaps investing in better delivery logistics, customer service training, product enhancements, or a loyalty program.

Step 2: Build Your Strategy

Identify the key success factors that you need to control in your business. Look at your current company, your competitors, and your customers. How can you build a business that meets the demands of your customers better than your competitors?

Start by looking at your competitive advantage. What differentiates you from others? What can you exploit? What can you do that others cannot copy immediately?

This should form a set of schemes, principles, and rules that are unique to your business, team, or you as an individual.

Something you can always come back to during times of uncertainty and hardship.

For executives planning their business milestones, ensure your strategy aligns to where you need to be going. It's very costly to spend time and energy fixing a business model that is no longer relevant.

Take the example of Blockbuster in response to Netflix in the late '90s. According to the story, instead of changing their business model to digital streaming, Blockbuster invested time, money, and energy to launch a DVD-by-mail rental service. A classic example of where it no longer makes sense to invest in a business model that had stopped meeting customer expectations—in this case, customers shifting toward streaming service versus a better DVD rental service.

We as humans are biased in building plans and strategies based on the realities of today, ignoring the possibilities of tomorrow. Regardless of the function you're in, a good exercise is to brainstorm where your customer is going. Whether you're a B2C company, a small B2B start-up, or a not-for-profit, find out what consumer expectations are changing and how you can meet them better than your competitors.

From a personal perspective, your strategy needs to account for how your business or role will evolve in a digital-first world by understanding: (1) where your business and/or industry is headed, and (2) what changes, pivots, and moves you'll need to make down the line as a result of disruption. This is true for anyone leading a company, taking on a new team, starting a new role, or trying to grow their career.

Step 3: Build Your Roadmap

Once you have your strategy, build a high-level map for getting to your destination.

Whether your objective is going to take three months, twelve months, or two years, list key milestones similar to destinations on a map that you want to hit over the course of your journey. This becomes your roadmap.

These are not to be confused with the actions you need to take or tasks that need to be completed in order to get there. That is too granular. Think of milestones as the "what" and actions as the "how." Focus on the "what."

For example, if my goal is to launch a new product in the next twelve months, then my milestones may include building a team, getting a product prototype ready, testing the product, and launching the product. Action items, on the other hand, would be things such as recruiting and interviewing candidates, training for the team and onboarding, sourcing the technologies, building testing plans, and communicating launch plans with key stakeholders, to name a few.

Some things to think about for your roadmap include who you might need on your team, what resources you might need, what obstacles you may need to counter, and how other projects and initiatives may impact your efforts.

Step 4: Build Your Off-Season Plan

Now, taking the key milestones in your roadmap, ask yourself what you need to do today to put yourself and/or your team in the best position possible to reach the end of your roadmap.

Let's break this into two parts—business and personal.

From a business perspective, this is where you identify the foundational elements that are crucial before you can start on your roadmap. Think of it as the behind-the-scenes work where you hire the right people or get buy-in. These are usually the basics, and oftentimes the most important.

For example, if your milestone from step 2 was to launch drone delivery, then a big behind-the-scenes step may be to learn and research as much as you can about drone delivery to make some key hires that come from that space. Or if your milestone was to build an omnichannel experience for your customers, then the foundational elements include upgrading your core technology that integrates with different services and systems down the road for added flexibility versus building on legacy tech and doing patch work. The latter is easier to do up front, but will pose numerous challenges in a changing future and will end up costing a lot more in time, effort, and budget along the way.

Your off-season plan is what you need to help you kick-start your strategy on the right foot and allow you to accelerate performance and maintain momentum throughout your roadmap.

From a personal standpoint, identify the things you must do in your first ninety days of embarking on a new role or project. These can include things such as building the right relationships, building personal systems and processes, or getting your personal work-life balance to a place where you're comfortable. Again, similar to the business points above, these are the basic things that you need to do to put yourself in the best position to perform. It's not complicated, but it takes effort and consistency.

These are also things you need to do daily to better prepare for your role. Preparing for meetings, motivating your team, and spending twenty minutes a week to better manage your time by taking a birds-eye view of everything that's going on.

Side Note:

A friend once told me that he hated his job and wanted to start his own business. I asked him what was stopping him. He said, "I don't have the time, and I can't afford to not get paid...I'm not lucky like you where I can spend time building something without getting paid for six months." Here's the thing—he had been complaining for three-plus years now. If he had spent two hours a week working on building his business and finding additional income streams, we wouldn't have been having this conversation.

I was fortunate to be surrounded by great people and support systems. And the reason I was able to afford to work on building my business and to write this book was because I built myself a playbook years in advance. I had put in the work, which provided me with enough savings, clients, and contingency plans to allow me to take risks. It wasn't luck.

In summary, as a leadership team, department head, or even a cross-functional project manager, identify the key actions that you need to take as a team to best prepare for the road ahead. What key investments will you need to make today to accelerate performance in the future? What technologies should you invest in today, or what systems need to be ripped and replaced? What bets should you make today to win in the future?

The remaining chapters will address how the foundational work will come into action and how you can execute on the specifics.

Exercise:

- Are you noticing any trends among your competitors' strategies or your customers' demands that could impact your positioning in five to ten years? How might that change your long-term strategy?

  ____

  ____

  ____

- What are some key foundational investments your business needs to make today for future success? What do you need to do today to remain competitive tomorrow and exceed customer expectations?

___

___

___

- What can you be doing daily to give yourself the best chance at peak performance?

___

___

___

CHAPTER 3

Build Superstar Teams

Superstar Team, Not a Team of Superstars

In 2010, the Philadelphia Eagles of the NFL finished the season with a 10–6 record. They had made the playoffs and were ranked the number two offense in the league. In 2011, to build on a great 2010 season, the Eagles made some bold moves in the off-season; it seemed like it was a do-or-die season for them.

They signed some really top-notch talent. These high-profile signings and contract extensions were shaping up to mold the Eagles into a force to be reckoned with. Michael Vick was signed to a new five-year contract extension worth $80 million. Nnamdi Asomugha, a veteran cornerback, was signed to a five-year, $60 million contract. Jason Babin, a defensive end, agreed to a five-year deal after a strong year where he was selected to the Pro Bowl (an NFL all-star team).

Ronnie Brown, a pro bowler from the Miami Dolphins,

also joined the team. Cullen Jenkins, a defensive end, signed a five-year $25 million contract. Vince Young, NFL rookie of the year from 2006 and a 2010 Pro Bowl selection, signed a one-year deal. He was signed to a $4 million contract as a backup quarterback after being cut by the Tennessee Titans. The roster had ten players who, when combined, counted for a total of twenty-five Pro Bowl selections. During a preseason press conference, Vince Young called the Eagles a "dream team."

The Eagles had high hopes of winning the Super Bowl and were considered by many as the favorites before the start of the season. They were the team that was expected to go all the way. The Eagles won the season opener 31–13 against the then St. Louis Rams. But what happened in the following weeks was shocking, to say the least.

The Eagles lost four straight games—games they were supposed to win according to the odds. They had a 4–8 record, with four games left in the season. "Dream team" sounded like a taunt by this point. The Eagles ended up winning the last four games of the season to finish with an 8–8 record. But it wasn't enough. They missed the playoffs after having made it to the postseason each of the previous three years.

How could a team perform worse than it did a year ago, despite adding a ton of great talent in an effort to win it all? Because they were unable to leverage the off-season.

The off-season is crucial in building chemistry and leadership in the locker room. But during the 2011 off-season, the NFL's collective bargaining agreement expired in March of 2011. The owners and the NFL Players Association could not agree to new terms, which resulted in a lockout of all team facilities and league operations. Players were not allowed to conduct team workouts and study sessions or to meet with the coaches. By the time a new agreement was reached on July 25, only a few days were left before teams opened training camps for the 2011 season.

Because many of the Eagles' players were brand new, the expiration of the NFL's collective bargaining agreement disproportionately impacted the Eagles' performance. So many of the new players on the Eagles were seeing each other for the first time during training camp. Unfortunately it was too late, and the team just didn't gel well enough in time.

The lack of a true off-season also impacted the execution of the plays. There just wasn't enough time for the players to learn and practice the new schemes to perfection. Each playbook is unique, and it takes time to get the execution down like clockwork. Teams count on having their starters back from the previous season, as they already know the systems and schemes. With so many new players, the team didn't get a chance to learn the systems until the start of training camp.

While a lack of chemistry and practice can be overcome with time, a key coaching change made it even tougher for the team to come together and respect the system. Juan Castillo was named the defensive coordinator for the 2011 season. According to media interviews, it was a decision that surprised many players as Juan had spent the previous thirteen years coaching the offensive line for the Eagles. It was rare to see an offensive line coach lead a defense in the NFL, which made it harder for some players to believe in the system.

In many of the media interviews months and years later, some of the players shared how different personalities just could not come together as one unit. There was a lot of strong leadership in the locker room. There were some great veteran players who had seen lots of prior success. But it was tough to get everyone to fit a system. The management went all in to try and win the Super Bowl, the coaching staff did the best they could despite the lockdown, and the players played their hearts out. But the Eagles never found that spark.

We've seen multiple examples of this across many sports teams. Some others that come to mind include the 2015 Dallas Cowboys, whom many believed were Super Bowl contenders as well, finished the season 4–12; or the New York Jets in 1996, who spent $70 million in the off-season to only finish the season 1–15; or Real Madrid in 2003, who only reached the Champions League quarter finals with a lineup that included Zidane, Luis Figo, Beckham, and Ronaldo. Money and resources do not guarantee championships. Alongside talent, you need a team that can work together, effectively.

In 2017, the Philadelphia Eagles did end up winning the Super Bowl. They beat the heavily favored New England Patriots. What was different this time? They played like a team! Ten of the starting twenty-two players were drafted over the previous five years. They had chemistry. They were on a mission. They were a superstar team, not just a team of superstars. Superstar teams win games on the basis of teamwork and grit, not talent.

Oh, and the 2017 Eagles won the Super Bowl with their backup quarterback, Nick Foles.

Concept:

To execute on your playbook, you're first going to need to build your team. A superstar team, or your "Olympic team," is a group of individuals working together and delivering results regardless of the challenges, uncertainties, or unforeseen circumstances. In other words, it is a team that is able to adapt, pivot, and adjust in order to achieve the overarching objective.

A superstar team is able to handle the demands of a fast-paced, highly disruptive, and changing future, day in and day out. It can consistently produce results without letting it take a toll on the overall morale of its people. There is minimal turnover on the team. When things get tough, they don't quit. Superstar teams always find a way to hunker down and push through adversity. A superstar team is not immune to failure, but it learns and gets better every step of the way. It bends but never breaks.

The speed of business today is fast, the fastest it's ever been. New technology and rising consumer demands are putting pressure on companies to adapt. Disruption is everywhere. The secret to handling competitive pressures, moving faster, being nimble, and taking decisive action starts with superstar teams. You can build an awesome strategic roadmap, source the best technology, and close some key clients. But none of it matters if your team is unable to follow through on your vision. You need a team that is able to execute and deliver results.

Superstar teams are not born. They are made. It takes focused planning, iterations, and adjustments. It takes a lot of crafting and hard work from the leader to mold it into a machine that can address the toughest business problems. Finding the right people, building a safe environment for your team to gel together, addressing early conflicts, and testing how the team handles pressure are all things a leader needs to do in order to build a strong team.

I've seen far too many leaders jump right into execution without building their teams and without putting in place the right measures to boost team performance. They get too fixated on doing things quickly and all by themselves, whether it's finding solutions, making decisions, or changing direction. And within a few months, they get burnt out. It doesn't matter if you're a CFO, director of supply chain, product manager, or a cross-functional lead, your success depends on your team.

Think about it; what is the cost of employee turnover each year? And how much more effectively does your team deliver results when everyone is aligned on your vision? Now, is it not worth spending a month or so up front to ensure that your team is positioned for success from the outset?

The fact that replacing a single team member results in two to four times their salary plus recruiter fees should be more than enough incentive to spend the time building and positioning your team to win. You don't want to be in the middle of a busy launch and have a key member of the team quit. The impact a single resignation has on your operations, timelines, and the team far exceeds any time you may have saved up front by jumping right into execution. Here are three core techniques or strategies for building teams that can win championships.

First is identifying and aligning to your system. I call it the systems-based approach. It means first identifying your system that you want to build, its purpose, and what it entails, and then finding the right people that fit the system. Your system is your business playbook from chapter 2. It differs depending on your roles and goals. The system for a leader in a digital transformation role for a large B2C company will look much different than for a CEO of a start-up looking to raise funding within the B2B space.

The systems based approach is about finding the right players that fit your system based on your goals, culture, industry, and competitive strategy, company life cycle, environment, and any other factors that influence your vision and mission. It's about identifying your destination and deciding who you need with you on the journey to maximize your chances of reaching your destination.

Second is hiring individuals for potential, character, and grit. There are numerous stories where a leader hired the best of the best, with a great résumé and top-notch skill set, but ended up failing. I've seen it happen firsthand, multiple times. A friend of mine was super excited with a recent hire she had made; the candidate showed promise given the caliber of companies he had worked for. But the candidate couldn't handle wearing multiple hats and the fast pace of execution, and within a few months he had completely checked out and stopped caring. Experience and talent will do you no good if the individual is not willing to work with others, go the extra mile, and do what it takes to win.

I believe it's better to hire someone with a mediocre skill set who brings great chemistry and diversity to the team versus someone with a spectacular résumé but a bad locker-room presence. Sports teams with strong players rarely fail to win due solely to a lack of talent. It's usually more to do with their locker-room presence, where egos get in the way. Therefore, it's up to the leader to ensure this doesn't become an issue when building the team. You never want to compromise the chemistry and morale of your team for a superstar who doesn't play well with others. Especially in a remote environment, it doesn't take much to ruin a team's culture or chemistry given how easily words and meanings get distorted over digital communications.

Side Note:

I was once on a cross-functional call, which also included a few of my own team members. It was during a busy week, and tensions were high. In response to a question from a peer, my team member answered in a frustrated, passive-aggressive tone. This isn't something I stand for, and I like to address it head-on. During the call, I first apologized to the person who asked the question, and then made it clear that there is no room for such behavior regardless of the circumstances. I recommended that both align after the call and discuss the underlying issues. It not only made subsequent calls smoother but also brought both of the team members closer and boosted productivity. If you leave this kind of behavior unaddressed, you'll very quickly see it spread throughout your organization. To prevent a negative locker-room vibe, address these issues head-on.

Lastly, a superstar team must complement a leader's management style and compensate for any weaknesses. If you have a servant-leadership approach for example, then the individuals that make up your team, regardless of the skill set, will be different from those reporting to an authoritative leader. I've seen mediocre teams skyrocket performance with a simple change in leadership. It all has to fit together. The individuals should also have skill sets that are not the strong suit of the leader. If you're building a new marketing team, and you're not the strongest in digital media buying, then someone on your team should possess that skill set (if that is required for where you're headed).

Sports to Business:

What can we learn about superstar teams from the world of sports? Let's use the example of a pro football team. A super team includes:

1. **System Talent Fit**
   A team with a talented group of individuals who want to win—most playbook schemes and systems are built around a few key positions, which are then enabled by everyone else around them by doing their jobs.

2. **Grit**
   A team that can weather tough losses and not self-implode. When a group of eleven tired, hurt, exhausted football players are on the field and need to make a big game-winning stop, grit is what allows them to find that extra bit of energy in the tank and leave it all out on the field.

3. **Respect**
   A team that believes in the system and leadership and respects each other. Respect is crucial to keep the team moving forward, together, during times of hardship versus finger-pointing.

4. **Chemistry**
   A selective group that fits the existing culture and brings a positive locker-room vibe, with great chemistry and no silos.

5. **High Standards**
   Having clear standards and guidelines for performance and conduct on and off the field. This stems from the leaders and must never be compromised.

In a business organization, a superstar team is one that can operate and deliver results like a well-oiled machine, ready to handle whatever comes its way. Similar to the football example above, this includes:

1. **System Talent Fit**
   Finding individuals who fit your system, leadership style, culture, and a role where they will have the opportunity to excel. Build the team around a few individuals who act as the glue and carefully align key support players to build on the positive culture.

2. **Grit**
   A team that can handle changes, pivots, and failures and continue moving forward. It's a group that hunkers down and rises to the occasion to battle adversity.

3. **Respect**
   Much like the football example, there must be respect for the leadership, each other, and the company. This is a must in order to weather moments of change and adversity.

4. **Chemistry**
   Teammates who have each other's back, keep the morale high when things get tough, and motivate each other to become stronger. There's no reason why a team that works remotely can't have the same type of chemistry as a football locker room.

5. **High Standards**
   Not tolerating any negative or toxic behaviors and addressing conflict head-on. It also means removing or

minimizing any negative politics, so the team can stay focused on getting results.

You want to build a SWAT team. A high-performing team. When projects across the company take a wrong turn, your team should be the team that gets called upon for help.

Action Plan:

Whether you have a few superstars on your team that don't play well together or you need to build a brand-new team, here is a five-stage process to building your "Olympic team."

Step 1: Current Team Alignment

Find out what your current team does well and what gaps exist. Is your team's genetic makeup, personnel, culture, and direction aligned to the system you are trying to build based on your overarching goals? Is the effort there? Are the results there? If the team is talented, are the results on par with expectations?

To figure out the gaps, try to spend time with your team. It's invaluable to sit beside your team and just observe the chemistry, interactions, and overall bond. It's definitely harder to do in a remote setting, but you should try having an "always on" Zoom room and designating hours where the team can be together while working on their tasks. If you are a senior leader, chat with those who don't directly report to you—direct reports of your direct reports. It helps you uncover how well aligned the entire team actually is on the vision, their understanding of what is expected from them, and any gaps that may exist. Summarize the gaps, whether it's gaps in your strategy, the system you're looking to build, or the team that is not aligned to the system.

One time I had a thirty-minute coffee chat with a team member who reported to one of my direct reports. It immediately uncovered significant alignment issues, which I addressed the very next day.

Step 2: Building the Team

Using the gaps from step 1, identify the hard and soft skill sets and key positions you need to hire for that fit your system, your culture, and your vision:

1. **System**
   Lay out your team structure—how everyone will work together and how the system will work. Plan the key roles you need, how they will interact with each other, internally and externally, and how each individual will support your strengths and complement your weaknesses as a leader.

2. **Culture**
   Map out the personalities you need, the ones you currently have, and how each individual will support the other. Look at the projects, the types of problems that may arise, and the requirements of each role. What kind of people would thrive in this environment?

Side Note:

Here is a personality table that I use, from a culture alignment standpoint. The personalities you need will vary from team to team. The roles in this table may also overlap across different individuals. The key is to ensure that you have the right mix of people to best support your playbook and the culture that you're building.

Personality Type	Description
Quarterback (vocal leader)	Well-rounded, natural leader who can influence and motivate others Able to make business decisions that keep the team moving in the right direction
Wide receiver (go-getter)	Highly talented or skilled individual in a specialist role Highly accountable and motivated by high-pressure situations
Lineman (supportive member)	A generalist who primarily works behind the scenes, does the heavy lifting Driven by the success of the collective team
Linebacker (tone setter)	A strong-willed, pace-setting individual who the team looks up to Loves to celebrate and feeds off of positive energy
Defensive back (empathetic leader)	A quiet individual who leads from behind High in EQ and empathy and keeps the team balanced during rough stretches

3. **Vision**
   Identify the types of values and traits that your team must embody based on your vision and where you're headed. The team needs to see and believe in your vision. These values and beliefs may depend on your vision, your goals, or types of projects.

But there are also certain values that I believe every team and leader should embody regardless of industry, project, or circumstances. These "uncompromising" values should always be front and center of your organization or team to bolster your execution amid disruption. These include:

- Being ethical: To never cut corners or do things that put your team in jeopardy
- Being human: To have compassion, empathy, and respect for one another
- Being humble: To always keep your ego in check and never think you're the best
- Being committed: Be committed to each other and to outworking your competition
- Being positive: To do the best you can regardless of situation or circumstances
- Being relentless: To see things through and quit only when finished

Without upholding these values in business, everything else (strategies, teamwork, tactics, etc.) will start to crumble.

Then actually go out and recruit. Recruit externally, internally, or reshuffle the teams, whatever the case may be. Recruiting is an art that I believe can really set a leader apart from his or her peers. It includes balancing a scientific approach with a people-first approach. It includes taking a chance on someone who has potential and character but lacks experience (with a backup plan if it doesn't prove to be a fit). It includes looking for candidates in unconventional places such as your recent guest lecture. You need to go beyond the traditional recruiting route.

Unfortunately, many people end up putting the effort in the wrong places, such as building job descriptions, and end up delegating much of the work to their HR counterparts. In my opinion, HR ends up doing 80 percent of the heavy lifting when the bulk of the work must be done by the team leader. It must be the leader's responsibility to find the best people for his or her team.

To build a superstar team, you cannot solely rely on HR. You cannot assume that the job posting will automatically get you the best candidates. A leader must always be building a pipeline of potential candidates through coffee chats, LinkedIn prospecting, and being open to connecting with those who reach out. After all, how can someone else, who doesn't fully understand your vision, your strengths, your gaps, and your intuition, find you the people that you need on your mission? Especially when the skill set that you need is changing every six to twelve months? Leveraging my pipeline, I was able to find four key hires in under two months because I worked hand in hand with my HR partners. It allowed us to find the right people quickly and kept everyone apprised of where we were headed as a team.

Step 3: Operationalizing the Team

In football, there is a big reset every year. It happens once when the off-season starts and once when training camp starts. The reset allows for the coaching staff to set key expectations on how to work together, set rules and parameters, clarify what the goals are and what the team is marching toward, and how to play as one team and one family.

As you build and upgrade your team per your system, it's important to reset and have an annual or semiannual kickoff where you set the new team in motion. A kickoff should be off-site if possible and should be designed to bring the team closer to each other with zero distractions. This kickoff is where you, as a leader, should set the tone. You should state key ground rules on how everyone will work together, align the team on the goals, set clear expectations, and get everyone bought in (something I cover in detail in chapter 5).

As a specific example of operationalizing the team, one thing that has worked well for me is using a one-page "onboarding document" that I build for all of my new hires during their first day of onboarding. It outlines the expectations of the role, how they will be evaluated, and how they will work with others through a scenario exercise. As per my team's feedback, it was the most helpful exercise I did as part of the onboarding. I use the onboarding document regardless of whether I have a new recruit or someone internal has come to my team. I also refer to it annually when resetting goals and realigning expectations.

Step 4: Consistent Communication and Iterations

Lastly, as you've aligned your team and your system of play and have kicked off and set the tone, remember to continue to communicate the key messages to your team and iterate as needed.

In your organization, set up weekly or monthly cadences to review performance, see what changes need to be made, and define clear next steps. This should be done as a team, regardless of rank, with full transparency. This is also when a leader reminds the team about the mission and alignment and determines if what the team is doing is working.

Ongoing checkpoints and iterations are highly dependent on how well a leader communicates to the team. Whether you're managing up, trying to influence your peers, or building a strong team and setting it in motion, you must over communicate. One of the biggest complaints I hear from my peers is the lack of communication and transparency. It's the leader's responsibility to ensure there is consistent, clear, concise communication within the team, both top down and cross-functionally.

For example, a direct report asks a question. The leader gets angry at the individual because the answer seems obvious to the leader. It isn't so obvious to the individual because there was no training provided and/or clear expectations were not established. As a leader, this is a great way to set yourself up for failure. It leads team members to eventually stop raising their hand, lose motivation, and mentally check out, resulting in lack of innovation and drive.

Most issues can be solved with proper communication, so tackle any issues head-on and maximize channels of communication. One thing that has worked for me is crafting my message without any assumptions. When putting together an email, an announcement, or before a one-to-one with a team member, I ask myself how my message would come across to the team or individual. Am I assuming certain things that only I know? Am I addressing what's most important to them? If I was in their role, what would I be interested in hearing, and how would I feel?

I also try to start each message with the "why" behind whatever I'm saying. It's a concept that has been discussed a ton and has been well articulated by Simon Sinek. Whether I need to motivate my team, share unfavorable news, or discuss a change, starting with the "why" makes it more transparent and keeps it human. Many times I share a story that makes it easier to see the "why," something I discuss in the later chapters of this book. When the "why" is clear, the how or the what becomes easy.

Step 5: Trigger Performance

Once the team is in place and has been mobilized, then it's time to put your team in the best possible position to win. First, start with understanding your team at an individual level. What motivates each of your team members, what are his or her strengths, and where do they need support?

Then identify if there are any shortcomings in each of the team members' abilities when it comes to team performance. Everyone has shortcomings, and it's a leader's responsibility to adjust and put each player in the best position to make plays. For any shortcomings, it's important to look beneath the iceberg and build a plan to address the issue. Try to identify the underlying issue, not just the symptom.

For example, if someone is not strong with external vendors and has a tough time keeping others on track to hit deadlines, it doesn't mean she isn't capable of managing projects. Perhaps the people on the project are much more senior and don't respect her decisions. So instead of training her on project and vendor management, you should instead coach her on building authority and commanding respect in cross-functional projects.

Lastly, once you've identified what drives each of your team members and where they play the best, now it's time to trigger performance. This starts with celebrating their wins, being there to clear any roadblocks, and giving praise and positive reinforcements. Of course, if someone is motivated by recognition, make sure to give them a shout-out during a team call. If someone is motivated by taking on harder problems, then keep increasing the challenge levels that you assign to this individual.

It comes down to understanding your team at an individual level, at a human level, outside the day-to-day formalities of a business. Above all, it takes commitment and focus from a leader to keep the team moving in the right direction.

Building a superstar team will help you conquer the tallest of the mountains, regardless of budgets, experiences, or unfavorable circumstances. Building a superstar team starts with your mindset as a leader. Invest in your team; the rest will come.

Exercise:

- What leadership style do you employ, and how can you further connect with your team at an individual level?

____

____

____

- Are you aware of the system you're trying to build and how your strengths will align to your team? Ask your boss, colleague, or friend about what they believe to be your top two or three strengths.

____

____

____

- How do you tolerate a——hole behavior in your team? If someone in your team is passive-aggressive on a call, is that normal, or is it addressed? What rules do you have in place for this?

____

____

____

CHAPTER 4

Build Adaptability

Anticipate Team Needs and Plan Ahead

I was putting together a digital transformation strategy for a global brand. My mandate was to transform the business to a digital-first company. In other words, drive digital sales growth and set up the right foundation for future success through technology. It included implementing new technology platforms, addressing interim gaps, streamlining and automating processes, bringing the key stakeholders along on the journey, and getting the right people on the bus to get us to the finish line.

The very first thing I decided to do was to build my team. My strategy was heavily influenced by something I had learned from Mark Verbeek, our strength and conditioning coach during my first three years at McMaster, who also served as one of our defensive line coaches.

For context, in the summer of 2010, during my second off-season, I realized that I may have to play two different positions in the upcoming season: nose tackle and defensive tackle. The nose tackle typically requires a heavier athlete (about 290 pounds), while the defensive tackle demands a slightly lighter player (about 270 to 275 pounds). I was about 275 pounds during the off-season and didn't plan to get heavier than 280 pounds because I would still need to play defensive tackle.

Therefore, in my off-season program prep meeting with Coach Verbeek, we discussed how I should best train to prepare for the upcoming season. At 275 pounds, I needed to get more powerful to play nose tackle without losing speed or agility. We started going through the base off-season workout program, reviewing it week by week.

Coach Verbeek decided to make a few adjustments. First, I would focus more on Olympic lifts to maximize my power and speed.[1] Second, for my weekly sprint sessions, he wrote "add a tire" beside the workouts in the booklet. So any sprint sessions I did, I used a harness to tie a tire behind me for added resistance.

Come regular season, as a result of Coach Verbeek's outcome-focused leadership approach, the third year was my best one yet. I played nose tackle and defensive tackle interchangeably and took on the full-time starting duties. I was selected to the East-West Bowl all-star game and won Defensive Lineman of the Year for McMaster.

---

1 Olympic lifting is a weight training method that entails moving a barbell with plates for maximum effort. Sets include a few (one to four) quick, powerful, and explosive reps. This method helps build power and speed, allowing an athlete to generate higher levels of force as compared to strength training alone.

Years later in the corporate world, as I was building my team, I had two options on how I could go about building a team that could execute the roadmap, stay focused, and adapt in changing environments.

The first option was the conventional approach that I had seen some leaders deploy, and something most of us are taught in school; hire really strong leaders who have done it before. Leaders who are experts in their field, who are specialists with numerous years of experience and have their ways of executing. This creates a potentially strong team that comes with a hefty price tag and may require significant time up front in recruiting the right people.

Alternatively, the second option was to build a team that was solely constructed for where we were headed and our end goal versus past success. In this option, it would be a matter of finding the people who could handle the journey ahead and not necessarily experts who've done it before.

Inspired by memories of Coach Verbeek's approach, I chose the latter option.

Where we were headed required speed, nimbleness, execution, and agility more than past success. The journey ahead was going to be full of changes and pivots. It meant finding people who were first and foremost adaptable, could work with each other, push through pivots, and could play multiple positions. It meant finding those who had demonstrated the ability to learn new things and solve problems that they hadn't seen before. I knew that the strategy would involve entering unknown territory and was something I wanted to build into the game plan from the start.

This doesn't mean I did not hire great people. A few of the key hires were really strong in their fields and could be called specialists.

But similar to Coach Verbeek, it meant finding and working with a team that could adapt and change as needed.

What did this team look like in action? It made some really big plays in a time span of under two years. We built and scaled a brand-new digital platform (ecommerce, app, loyalty, and analytics engine), upgraded hundreds of locations with brand-new technology in record time, boosted the app store rating from 1+ to 4+ stars, and saw over 65 percent increase in digital sales.

The most important accomplishment, however, was one of team morale. It was the only team with zero turnover in its first year despite the pivots, turns, and ups and downs.

Concept:

To ensure success in a disruptive, uncertain, and changing world, you need to hire, build, and train for adaptability. Over the next decade, the ability to change, pivot, and execute in an ever-changing environment is a must for leaders and their teams in order to grow in the coming years. Building adaptability can be summed up as the ability to continuously adapt to the long-term needs of the business. This applies to an individual, a team, and an organization.

As of the mid to late 2000s, business models have been

shifting. Most businesses have found, or are desperately trying to find, new lines of business. A business model, in simplistic terms, refers to how a business makes money. Most businesses are now shifting from traditional to "digital" business models, where the transactions of goods or services happen over the internet. Examples of this include e-commerce, Instagram shopping, online ordering and pickup, virtual appointments, and so forth.

The competitive advantage that made certain companies enjoy strong market holds for decades is now eroding. As a result, the value chain of a typical business has changed substantially. Many businesses in the '90s and early 2000s grew on the basis of R&D, proprietary technology, and first mover advantage. These are no longer sufficient. Yes, we can argue that Netflix, Amazon, and Starbucks, all leaders within their spaces, have the best technology and consumer experiences. But their core strength lies in having their internal capabilities aligned to best support where the consumer is going. Being great in managing change and adaptability. This is further explained in later chapters, which highlights the drivers behind the shift. But in summary, the competitive advantage that allows businesses today to continue growing amid disruption has shifted toward leadership and adaptability.

These days, a company known for being the best in TV ads no longer matters given the rise of social media and digital ads. Having the best retail location doesn't help unless your online experience matches your in-store experience. This means that especially for larger, traditional businesses, individual capabilities, training, systems, and methods of execution in marketing are falling out of alignment from what is required to thrive in the new world.

If your business is diverging into multiple lines of business and digital revenue streams, then a marketing team that is superb in direct mail and TV ads is great. But it also needs to have capabilities with a baseline understanding of executing paid digital ads to better reach your customers, such as Instagram ads and influencer collaborations.

But that's not the main point.

Because we live in a world that is changing so fast, upskilling your team or onboarding new talent alone to better manage digital ads won't help. Why? There is a high likelihood that AI (artificial intelligence) and automation will be able to execute all digital marketing campaigns in the next five to ten years. This means your team that has learned to manage digital ads will have to relearn and adapt yet again to the new way of managing digital marketing.

What will that look like in the next five to ten years? Possibly managing AI and holistic marketing strategy, while letting AI and automation handle the execution and analysis of digital marketing ads.

Net-net—the team must be adaptable, and leadership must recognize and prepare.

Since the 2020 pandemic, here are a few common trends across industries that have accelerated the need for future adaptability:

- Consumers expect the best of the best experiences and have a very low tolerance for friction.
- It's easier to compete across industries with the availability of cost-effective tech solutions. Predictive analytics, online ordering, and process automation are becoming table stakes.
- Over the next decade, advances in AI will make technology skills a commodity, eroding most tech-based competitive advantages. This will increase automation, allowing for a higher number of new entrants and disruption.
- Leaders only have a finite number of hours per day, and the number of decisions needed to be made on a daily basis is increasing.
- Innovation is continuing to grow exponentially, and the number of derivatives as a result is only increasing.
- Disruption is to become a norm, with big giants going on acquisition sprees to build capabilities to enter new markets that were once outside their reach.

Therefore, the core capabilities that most leaders need to build to sustain and grow over the next decade will become the ability to change, adapt, pivot, and execute in an ever-changing environment. The best organizations will simply shift and adapt their execution to the new strategy, and great leaders will be able to prepare their teams with the right capabilities needed for the near future.

Sports to Business:

In pro sports, there are baseline requirements for a player to be selected to join a team. This baseline is determined by (1) physical requirements to perform at the level of current elite athletes and (2) fitting into the team's system, playbook, and style of play.

To break it down further, every football team in the NFL or the CFL may have the following three baseline requirements at an individual level:

1. **Physical Capability**
   Everyone on the team must have a certain level of physical capability—size, strength, speed, talent, and agility. There's a baseline needed to perform and add value to the team. It's a physical game, and it requires the players to be able to run, be athletic, hit, and at times, take a hit. So everyone must be able to do the basics.

2. **High-Pressure Thinking**
   There has to be a certain level of critical thinking ability. Football is as much a mental game as it is physical. Hundreds of different schemes, half-time adjustments, audibles, playing different positions, and picking up changes quickly under pressure, among other things, are taking place in every game. This requires a player to have a certain level of mental focus in high-pressure situations.

3. **Value Alignment**
   Every player must align to the team's values. This is also known as the locker-room presence. Unfortunately, not every team gets it right, and at times it's something that's put on the back burner. We've seen numerous stories where a team signs a really talented player, who ends up bringing a bad locker-room vibe. This hurts the entire team.

Every year, major sports leagues have an entry draft where teams select eligible college athletes in their senior years. Leading up to the draft, there is some sort of a pro evaluation camp to better evaluate the players in a controlled setting. These camps or "combines" consist of predefined physical tests that each player has to perform. In the NFL combine, for example, some of these tests include a bench press evaluation and a standing broad jump.

Now, some prospects who had a great season at the college level may get drafted despite a poor performance at the combine. However, it's more likely that someone with a great combine performance will get drafted despite a mediocre college season performance.

Why? Because teams are focused on finding players that have an underlying level of skill set and athletic abilities required to play in the NFL. It's about the core capabilities that a player brings to the team in order to thrive in the future (a.k.a. the ability to adapt).

Now, you may say that the football analogy above doesn't have much to do with anticipating new future capabilities. Other than becoming better at the physical skill set and executing the systems, the actual rules of football don't change all that much. You're 100 percent correct.

That is precisely why in a digital-first world today, this concept is even more critical. The requirements, business models, and competitive forces will continue changing. As leaders and organizations, we will continuously need to adapt.

This means leaders must strive to build a baseline capability level for employees that allows them to adapt and thrive in the future. Specifically, through the following:

1. **Digital Readiness**
   This is a basic fundamental understanding of tech and tools required to compete and perform on the role. As individuals, it is being able to make sense of the technologies and systems to become more effective and efficient. As an organization, it's about having teams that are positioned to exploit the digital technologies of the future.

2. **Execution and Adaptability**
   This is the ability to learn new things, take risks, iterate, make quick decisions, change direction, pivot, and sustain momentum in uncertainty. Given everything is cross-functional, this also includes building the capability to work across departments, challenges, and disciplines, while having influence as needed.

3. **Values**
   It's important to have individuals that align to the value of the business and where the business is going. Change and adapting to the future require a certain attitude, and conflicting value systems will make it harder for individuals to follow through with the needs of the business.

Action Plan:

Regardless of where you are on your journey, here is a four-step process to getting started on building adaptability to position yourself and/or your business for growth over the next few years.

Step 1: Identify Your Future Position

Before you can build the capabilities of the future, first identify where you want to go. In chapter 2, we discussed identifying your future competitive position. This adds a people lens to it. The key is to identify your vision and long-term position from a people capability standpoint.

The best place to start is with your organization's top-level three-to-five-year strategic plan—what are the key areas you want to play in, competitors to fend off, macro-environment forces or legislations to combat, new products to launch, who to acquire, etc.? Based on this plan, what kind of capabilities will you need in the future from a people standpoint?

You can also spend time watching your competitors or other businesses who are pioneers in their areas. Watch where they are headed from a consumer and competitive positioning standpoint. Then go a level deeper to see how they are preparing to adapt. What kinds of skill sets are they hiring for? What kinds of training are they conducting? What kinds of roles are they building? The more you analyze, the better you can predict.

As an individual, where do you want to be in the next two to four years? What kinds of roles or industries do you want to dominate in? You can study the environment around you. You can also watch where your colleagues and industry leaders spend their time. What kind of capabilities is someone who is two to three levels above you investing in? What are some of the hard and soft skills that you see your mentors embody? Analyze and build yourself a future vision.

Step 2: Identify Current Baseline

Look at your current team and evaluate your team from a digital skill set, adaptability, change-readiness, and value-alignment perspective. Identify which of these capabilities exist today and map out the gaps between today and where you need to be from step 1.

One thing that helps when we conduct this exercise with some of our clients is separating any specialist positions from generalist positions. Specialist positions will have a lower need to adapt or change from a competency standpoint as compared to generalists such as project managers or strategic consultants. Separating these roles will allow you to identify gaps that make more sense for each role or department.

Similarly, as an individual, evaluate where you stand in terms of personal adaptability and alignment to your future vision. What gaps exist today? For example, if you're looking to enter a new industry given its future attractiveness, what kinds of skill sets do you need to acquire, or what might you need to do that is outside your comfort zone?

Step 3: Build a Capability Plan

Now take the gaps from step 2 and build a two-pronged plan, one for internal capability training and one for external capability acquisition.

For example, let's say you predicted from step 1 that your business is highly susceptible to tech giants who are looking to enter your market and offer similar products or services. For you to defend your market share against these new entrants, it may require an innovation team and the need to promote a fail-fast culture, as well as vertically integrate closer to the customer for faster time to market. Then in step 2, if you identified that you lack internal capability for most of these areas, build a plan that includes training and upskilling your current team. It could also include a plan for external talent acquisition to help you close the gap over the next twelve to twenty-four months.

For internal capability, this can include things such as workshops, courses, off-sites, etc. to help your current organization build the skills to become more adaptable. For external capability acquisition, it's about hiring individuals with a skill set that may be hard or too costly to teach internally. This should include talent that comes from an environment where adaptability was a must.

Personally, identify two to three key investments you should make to help you close the gap and become more adaptable.

Side Note:

I spend thirty minutes a week working through a case study, because I believe conceptual and analytical problem-solving are my competitive advantage. I try to find real problems across the business world, such as a business deciding on a new direction, an executive looking to improve team productivity, or a business addressing poor product performance. For each case, I work on identifying the root cause behind the underperformance and determining the key levers that I would use to solve the problem. This regular practice allows me to hone my critical thinking, decision-making, and problem-solving skills.

Step 4: Operationalize and Evaluate

This is where the rubber hits the road. Once you've created a plan, now it's time to execute. Work with your colleagues to build the training programs and seek buy-in if needed from the leadership team. Build a talent acquisition strategy with your HR team that you can execute over the coming months for external talent.

With effective execution, the results will speak for themselves. Some positive signs of adaptability will include the following:

- People are able to play multiple positions.
- People are able to execute on projects without prior experience (assuming, of course, there are no licensing requirements at play such as lawyers, engineers, etc.).
- There is less pushback to changing demands.
- There will be less reliance on external talent over time.
- The team morale is higher.

Personally, hold yourself accountable to follow through with the key investments you need to make from step 3. For example, you can add your plan to your annual calendar, share your plan with your spouse or a friend to keep you accountable, or add it to your weekly routines.

Every six months, as you execute, repeat steps 2 and 3 to ensure you're moving in the right direction. This is a continuous process.

Exercise:

- If you were to time travel five years into the future, do you believe your team today has the right skills and capabilities to compete in that future? If not, what gaps might you need to fill?

____

____

____

- How can you or your team better accept change and adapt to new technologies? What are some biases or beliefs that are holding you back? (This is one that many of our clients bring up, and oftentimes it's due to lack of communication and training.)

  ____

  ____

  ____

- What is one personal skill or ability that you would like to acquire to better position yourself in the future? What steps can you take today to get there?

  ____

  ____

  ____

CHAPTER 5

Get System Buy-In

Don't Quit on Me; I Won't Quit on You

It was Thursday night before the Canadian Thanksgiving weekend in October 2011, and we had just secured a victory at home at Ron Joyce Stadium at McMaster University. As the game clock hit zero, we made our way to the middle of the field, shook hands with the rival team, and jogged back to the far side of the field for a quick huddle with our coaches.

Any other night we would have gone straight into the locker room and sung our victory song. But since we were going away for the long weekend, the only long weekend during the football season, our head coach had called for a huddle on the field. He wanted to make use of whatever focus we had left after the long game before we started tapping into long weekend mode.

It was a short huddle. Coach P and positional coaches went over the plan for the coming week and wished everyone a happy

Thanksgiving. At the end Coach P said, "Enjoy the time off with your family. Cherish it. Enjoy it. You've earned it. Great season so far, and I'm proud of each and every one of you."

As we were about to stand up and do our final breakdown, Coach P pointed to the stands behind him. Most of the spectators had left, and like any other home game, the ones who stayed behind in the stands were our families and friends. Wearing our maroon and gray team colors, they were slowly making their way to the lower level of the stadium to cheer us on once we made our way toward the locker room. While still pointing at the stands, Coach P slowly turned back and looked us in the eyes. And then he smiled, his eyes lit up, and in an exciting tone, he said, "I can't wait to be back here next week with all of you! Come Sunday, kiss your mom and girlfriend goodbye. Hug your families because we're going back to work. And it's going to be a long few weeks!"

Now, for someone to hear this who has no context of the season, the players, or what happened during that season, it may sound like a harsh thing to say on the eve of Thanksgiving. But for all the players and coaches, it was exactly what we needed, and frankly, all that we wanted to hear.

In 2011, we were a team that knew this was our year to shine. No one on the team had ever made it to our conference finals. We were the underdogs. But we knew we could do it. We knew this was our shot at defying odds and making history. So as excited as Coach P was to come back and be with the team after Thanksgiving, we were just as excited and wouldn't have it any other way.

This was what the seniors on the team had bought into four years ago during our rookie training camp, and then again during off-season training, and then again the next year, and the year after. Every workout, every practice, every nutrition seminar, every class, every up and down, and despite every loss, we had bought into working hard to give ourselves a shot at winning the league title.

On the eve of Thanksgiving in 2011, this was a team that was fully committed to their vision, the coaching staff, their goals, the systems, and above all, into each other.

This brings us to the concept of system buy-in.

Concept:

For a team to deliver in an ever-changing environment, face setbacks, and persevere through hardships, it needs to have a strong belief into the what, the how, and the why. System buy-in is one of the simplest, but arguably the most powerful and overlooked, concepts among business leaders today. System buy-in is where a team as a collective unit, as well as the unique individuals that make up the team, believe in a shared vision, buy into each other, and are marching together toward something more than just a paycheck.

In digital environments, where the industry is moving fast and teams are dispersed and fragmented, delivering results is hard. There are a lot of pivots with lots of iterations, and sometimes things don't pan out. Which means that a leader needs his or her team to be resilient and able to handle adversity, day in and day out. A team that is fully bought into the leader's vision will keep marching forward, with a lower likelihood of doubting, finger-pointing, and quitting.

One cannot expect leaders to achieve earth-shattering results in a world of uncertainty with a group of people who don't believe in where they're going. Before any major endeavor, buy-in has to be the number one priority if we are looking to maximize the chances of long-term success.

Furthermore, in this world with finite attention spans, limited time, and bombardment of new tech and innovation, it's imperative for leaders to maximize their impact and influence in order to accelerate performance in the new world of speed and uncertainty. And the only way a leader can maximize performance is if the team has bought into the vision, goals, mission, and above all, into the leader.

A team that fully buys in is less vulnerable to disruption. The primary goal then becomes getting to the finish line, regardless of the obstacles in the way. And any changes in direction, or things going sideways, simply become roadblocks that need to be jumped over or run through. Buying in makes it about achieving the "end" without worrying about the "means."

I've held roles across companies that were generally held by people much more senior than me in age and experience. In addition to getting my own team on board and aligned, it came with an added challenge of convincing those who didn't report to me to buy into my vision and treat me as an equal.

I knew that trying to prove to everyone that I deserve to be there due to my skills, education, or my ability to drive change wasn't going to cut it. I instead focused on showing what the vision was, how it would benefit everyone collectively, and what it would mean to win. That was all that people really wanted to hear. It starts with a shared vision, not data, stats, or authority.

Side Note:

I once had to deliver news to a group of business owners that their business model was about to change. They would be taking home less money and had no power to change or negotiate. Additionally, I had to get them to sign the new contracts on the spot.

Some of these operators had been in business since before I was born. As a young manager, I wasn't sure what to do. So I just shared what I knew at the time with full transparency and honesty. I told them that I did not know what was going to happen, but I was going to do whatever I could to help them navigate through the change. Instead of being fixated on the details of the change, the metrics, and why the company was making this move, I focused my conversation on getting through this uncertain period together.

To my surprise, that was what they wanted to hear. Everyone signed, with no pushback.

Sports to Business:

System buy-in is at the core of any successful championship sports team. It's the most fundamental principle that dictates whether a team can manage uncertainty and find a way to win in the face of adversity. Taking the example of a football team, the individual players and the team all need to buy into the following three things:

1. **Believing in the Off-Season Workout Program**
   No team wins a championship with just a few months of practice. Championships are won based on the preparation and work a team puts in during the off-season. So the bulk of the foundational strength and conditioning work happens during a grueling off-season. What makes it so tough isn't just the intensity of the workouts, but the fact that there are no more coaches yelling at you to motivate you, there are no more teammates who push you for that one extra rep. It becomes very easy to slack off and skip a few reps.

   But good players know that if they're to give their team the best chance at winning when the season starts, they need to prepare with all they've got when no one is watching. That is what gives them the edge. Over time it adds up.

   We were lucky to have most of the team local over the summer holidays, which meant we were able to have a few weekly gym and field work sessions as a team.

   And the workouts were grueling. Getting through a three-hour workout at seven in the morning on Sundays during the summer was not mandatory but something we all bought into. We knew it was going to be worth it in the end. We had to believe in it as a team.

2. **Buying into the System and Coaching Staff**

This is big. A team that does not buy into the system, playbook, and coaching staff's ability to call plays will never win a championship.

Why? When the game is on the line, there is absolutely zero room for doubt. If even one player does not execute per the plan and misses his or her assignment, good teams will exploit that gap and do some damage. Once we bought into our system and into our coaches, it didn't matter what play was called and whether or not we all agreed if it was the best call. We had full faith, and we respected the call. We would commit and execute to the best of our ability and focus on what we were all responsible for.

3. **Believing in Each Other**

Sports are an interesting dynamic. As players you compete against your teammates for the starting spot, but at the same time you need to have each other's back during game day. It all starts with believing in the team and treating each other like family.

It's absolutely required to go all out in training camp and to be competing with your teammates. That is what pushes a team to get better as a unit. But off the field, outside the drills, and come game day, great teams and leaders have each other's backs and play unselfishly for something much bigger than their starting spot.

In a business setting, regardless of where a leader is on organizational journey in this digital age, system buy-in means that the team buys into the following:

1. **Buy into the leader**

   A leader's number one priority must be his or her team, and in this case it means having the team buy into his or her vision and capability as a leader. Getting the team to believe in the mission always comes before execution, strategy, presentations, hard skills, or anything else.

   Having a team buy into the leader doesn't mean they have all the answers or know how to do everyone's job. It simply means they're open, honest, can show vulnerability, and will find a way to get things done in partnership with their team. It means the team will follow the leader on the mission and trust the leader's ability to lead them.

   Sometimes a leader expects the team to buy in without creating a space that is safe and open. I've been on both sides of the ball and heard countless stories from colleagues and friends about toxic leadership—bosses expecting their teams to do certain things but with little to no effort on building a safe environment and earning the team's trust. This is a recipe for failure.

Trust and respect in the leader are important in environments where decisions need to be made quickly and things are chaotic. Seldom do we agree with 100 percent of the decisions a leader makes or what we're asked to do in a certain role. That diversity is what builds strong teams. But in times of uncertainty, of immense pressure, such as during a product launch failure, a last-minute change request two hours before an executive presentation, or a PR crisis, sometimes it makes sense for a leader to call the play from an authoritative standpoint. It happens in big games, and it happens in business. And what separates teams that commit and execute on an order versus those who question and push back is their level of buy-in to the leader. It doesn't matter if the team doesn't feel great about the chosen strategy, but if there is respect and trust in the leader, the team will execute.

Side Note:

I was overseeing a really large implementation across more than a thousand locations for a global brand. Unfortunately, the systems and tech that we were rolling out kept crashing, and it always happened during the weekends. I was working long days during the week. Then on the weekend, I would have to be on calls all day, coordinating, troubleshooting, and managing expectations. This continued for a few months, where I worked almost every weekend.

One Sunday, I was questioning whether any of it was worth it. I could be doing less work and getting paid the same or more somewhere else. The CIO at the time had an open-door policy and was very approachable, so I booked a meeting with her to tell her how I felt. It was a simple conversation, but she reminded me about the "why" and helped me buy into her vision. Those thirty minutes were absolutely worth it. We ended up stabilizing the systems and completed the rollout in record time. The experience I gained during those few months is invaluable. It helped me lead and deliver large deployments years later. Had the CIO not created an environment of trust, the results would've been very different.

2. **Buy into the company**
   This is what hurts most leaders and makes it harder to satisfy point one above. The team needs to buy into your company's overall vision and values. You can be an amazing leader, but if your team doesn't believe in the company's overall direction and leadership, then it's a lot tougher for them to buy into your vision. Some of this is a product of hiring the right people (covered in chapter 3), and the other half a product of communication and aligning expectations at the start.

3. **Buy into each other**
   Business teams are made up of people just like you and me. If your team spends over eight hours a day together,

then it might as well be for something more than a paycheck. Great teammates drive each other, motivate each other, and make it a fun environment. In fact, a big proponent of delivering spectacular results as a team despite unfavorable circumstances is when individuals respect and care for the success of each other and want to see everyone succeed.

Buying into each other brings forward transparency, room for growth, and innovation. You can hire the best of the best, but if they don't believe in each other, then you'll have a hard time executing as a leader.

Action Plan:

First of all, nothing matters if you don't believe in your mission. So ask yourself the following questions:

- Do you believe in your company's vision and the tasks assigned to you?
- Do you believe the company's values align well to your internal values?
- Are you happy with where you're headed in your career?

If you answered no to any of these questions, you need to have a tough conversation with yourself. Either you'll need to find a way to buy in and commit to your current organization regardless of circumstances, or you'll have to make a change, either within the organization or to something new. Because before you can have someone believe in you, you need to first fully believe in where you are headed. Otherwise, thriving in a disruptive world and trying to get teams to deliver when things go sideways is going to take a lot more effort.

Once you've answered the questions above, here is a four-step action plan that you can implement.

Step 1: Make It Personal

Understand your team at an individual level. Although it's a hard combination to have your team respect you, believe in your leadership, and at the same time be able to crack jokes and see your personal side, it's something every great leader needs to strive for.

The only way you can have all three is by getting to know your team at an individual level. What does each member want out of this job and out of their career? What motivates them? What are their strengths? What would make them believe in your vision?

If you can go as far as building a spreadsheet with each team member's name and, for each, writing down their personal goals, career goals, motivational styles, and strengths, that would be a strong first step. This will help you build a map of what your team is looking for at the most fundamental level and how you as a leader need to serve your team so that everyone can buy into your vision.

A unique thing about most sports teams is that most players have a nickname. It's like a badge of honor to have a nickname. It means the coaches and teammates "get" you at an individual level. There is something special you bring to the team.

Three days into my first college football training camp, I had a nickname: Gooey. It was "assigned" to me by our defensive line and strength and conditioning coach Mark Verbeek. I was known as Gooey from that day onward. All of my teammates to this day still call me Gooey. I never really found out the reason behind the name, but I think it had something to do with my flexibility, long arms, and my last name. Point being, football coaches and teammates treat each other as family, not just a number. So find out who your people are and why they should believe in your mission.

Step 2: Share the Why

The "why" is always the same: to get better every day and win a championship. You must show your team that their job is more than just coming to work and getting paid—it's about achieving the unachievable, it's about defying odds, it's about proving others wrong who didn't believe in you. And above all, it's about proving to each other that you're capable of much more. Every single day, at every single milestone, especially when you hit a wall and things don't go your way, it's imperative that you remind your team about the why. The North Star.

Grueling off-season workouts, long training camps, tough road-game stretches, close losses, injuries, and for some, playing their last game of competitive football ever—the only thing that keeps a sports team moving forward is that North Star, that light at the end of the tunnel. And it is the coach's responsibility to ensure the team sees it.

How you communicate your "why" is also important. It must be communicated with excitement, through emotions, and with a powerful, positive, and forward-looking tone. So tell a story, share your personal why, and show some excitement as you get your team aligned to the North Star!

Step 3: Be a Role Model (Actions over Words)

In digital-first, dispersed teams, flattened-structure environments, preaching "the what" seldom ever works. Instead you need to become the reason why others should follow by simply modeling the right behaviors, rituals, and practices.

It's important to find ways to show you don't just talk, that you do the work. Show your team you're there to remove their obstacles. Show that you'll be on video calls late if your team is working well into the evening. Go to bat for your team regardless of how big or small the issue is. Be there for your team. That is your job as a leader. Enable your team. In return, your team will strive to never let you down.

Side Note:

A colleague of mine came to me one day and started complaining about how her team wasn't showing any sense of urgency and how they didn't seem very motivated. It was a few weeks before a deliverable, where the business was announcing a new partnership. I asked her what the root cause might be, and she mentioned that they just didn't care. Then on a different topic, she started explaining how she didn't believe in the direction that the leadership was going toward and was updating her résumé. A few minutes later, she connected the dots.

Stage 4: Open Your Perspective

As you start managing people at an individual level, getting your team aligned on your "why," and modeling the right behaviors, you might also at times need to shift your perspective.

No one knows everything. Strategies change, more so than we think, especially in today's world. Therefore, having open dialogue with your team, listening to their suggestions, and truly enabling each other means at times a leader needs to change his or her ideals or way of doing things.

What worked last year, or a tactic that worked great with a different group of people, may not work with your current team or in your current situation. Therefore, getting buy-in comes with earning respect, and one way to earn respect is to truly listen to your team and execute in alignment. Together.

Listening to your team and shifting your perspective will earn you respect. And for times when you do need to make a call that the team doesn't fully support, as long as there is respect, the team will execute to the best of its ability.

Step 5: Build a Community

As you start getting buy-in, build a close-knit community. Building a community that believes in the vision and everyone involved in the journey will help you conquer the biggest of challenges. Building a community helps you align the team on a common goal. It allows them to grow their level of commitment organically and holistically. It builds a culture with a strong sense of purpose for the collective team. During times of change and hardships, the community will help your team maintain its level of buy-in and commitment to you, to the company, and to each other.

Why do pro athletes or elite military soldiers push through the hardest of challenges as part of the selection process? What pushes them to see things through despite the grueling experiences? It's because they want to be a part of a community that is only reserved for very few people. They want to be a part of a movement. It allows teams to uphold high standards, deliver on commitments, and hold each other accountable.

Side Note:

During the rollout of an app, I needed about ten to fifteen volunteers to help us test internally before we launched it on the App Store. During our initial calls for volunteers, no one stepped forward. A few weeks later, I made an announcement to everyone at the client's office that we were looking for people to join us on a new "digital innovation team" that we were building. They would be the first ones to see the new app, would be able to test and provide feedback, and would contribute to the overall launch. Oh, and I said, "We only have room for five people." We ended up getting more than double that number to sign up. We accepted everyone who signed up for the new digital innovation team.

Exercise:

- List all the things that you're doing today to get your team to believe in you as a leader. What is working and what's not working? For example, are you seeing less resistance, is your team more committed to your vision, and does your team respect your decisions? What can you do differently?

  ____

  ____

  ____

- Refer back to the action plan from this chapter. If you believe you're not committed to your mission, what are some steps that you can take today to change that? What can you do to better buy into your organization, or what changes can you make in your career?

  ____

  ____

  ____

- What is the "why" behind your vision and all that you do? How can you get others to believe in it? Think in terms of storytelling and excitement—get creative.

  ____

  ____

  ____

In this section we've identified and formed a plan to build and strengthen the foundations needed to thrive in a disruptive future. The next section will focus on how to execute and implement in the face of uncertainty, change, and chaos.

SECTION 2

Regular Season: Execute and Implement

P—Postseason
R—Regular season
O—Off-season

CHAPTER 6

Put On Your Headphones

Block Out the Noise

The sports mindset has helped pull me out of situations where I had my back against the wall.

It was just after six in the evening. I was sitting at my desk in an empty, silent office, with my head in my hands, panicking.

I was leading a digital transformation project for a global company. The project had an aggressive timeline with little margin for error. Four months in, we were blindsided by something totally unexpected, and our entire roadmap derailed. I should've seen it coming, but I didn't. All the resources, hard work, and effort we had put in was all wasted. Gone.

I remembered how disappointed and sad the team felt when I announced that we'll have to make a complete pivot, and everything we had done so far didn't matter. The mission we were about to abort was a big reason why the team had decided to join me on the journey.

I could feel others in the organization starting to doubt the roadmap, the plan, and, in part, my leadership and the execution of my team. It's hard enough to earn the trust of your team, let alone the partners and colleagues in a large global company.

All to say there was a lot of noise, and I didn't know how to control it. I didn't see a way out. In a way I was feeling sorry for myself. The victim mentality. I was questioning my decision to have taken this role. *Maybe they were right*, I thought. *You're too young for this. You're not ready. You don't deserve this.*

To break away from this negative self-talk, I asked myself, "If this was a football game, what would you do?"

More specifically: "What would you do if someone blind-sided you on the football field? Would you lie there on the turf feeling sorry for yourself, playing the victim card, complaining to the referee about the hit?"

And at that moment, I had a flashback to when Michael "Pinball" Clemons came to speak to our football team. Michael is the general manager of the Toronto Argonauts, a six-time Grey Cup champion and a CFL legend. He is a five-feet-six, retired, award-winning football running back with numerous records to his name. And he's the most energetic person you'll ever meet.

During the 2011 season, we were going through our final run-through the day before our conference final Yates Cup match. At the end of the run-through, we saw Michael come out of the tunnel. He made his way toward the huddle with that large, infectious smile and gave us one of the best football speeches I've ever witnessed.

Toward the end of his talk, he stopped and looked at us, each and every one of us, deliberately. It felt as if he was asking us to make a promise. Then he said the one thing that carried us through the playoffs:

> *"Every man, every play, every down, all day."*
> *"Every man, every play, every down, all day."*
> *"Every man, every play, every down, all day."*

He said it thrice and had us repeat it together a few more times. A group of hungry, sweaty, underdog football players all repeated it like a chant that you could hear on the other side of the campus.

Every man, every play, every down, all day. He didn't have to explain what it meant. It was clear. Everyone on the team, showing up, ready to go, giving it their best, and never taking a play off. Consistently.

That's all you have to do, and that's all you can control—show up consistently and execute.

Thinking back to that moment with Pinball Clemons when I was stuck, I found the answer I needed.

What happened to my roadmap was unfortunate, and there was a lot of noise out there. Noise in my head, noise from the team, noise from the business. There were doubts. But all that I could do at this point was to show up, block out the emotions, and execute. That's it. All I could do was to objectively align on a new path and get to work. No more complaining, playing the victim card, or making up excuses.

That mindset changed everything. The next morning I showed up with a completely different perspective. I focused on three things.

One, I blocked out all the noise. I stopped worrying about what happened, what others might think, or whether people still believed in my roadmap. Instead, I focused on what I could control and executed it to the best of my ability.

Two, I let data and facts drive my actions, plans, and decisions. It helped me take a step back from the situation and execute based on whatever was in front of me.

Lastly, I reminded my team about the "why" behind what we were doing. When we had signed up for this project, we knew it wasn't going to be easy, and this roadblock was something we would overcome.

As I shifted my mindset, my team followed suit shortly after. A few months later, we were back on track. Things started falling into place.

Fast-forward a year, we executed some of the most successful projects in record time. In fact, we had a few of our major vendor partners ask us about the secret behind our speed and precision despite our small size, so that they could share best practices with their larger clients.

I told them it was simple. "Focus on what you can control. And execute."

Concept:

When you start making big plays, you'll need to stay focused and not let distractions affect your performance. Putting your headphones on is about staying focused on the task at hand and blocking out the noise. It's about not letting the negativity or noise slow us down. In today's world, we are bombarded by information, feedback, data, opinions, judgment, social media, etc. Because good things take time and the speed of execution is much faster today, mistakes, iterations, and ups and downs are part of the process. Therefore, it is super important to stay focused in a world that is always on "loud."

There are two main drivers of noise in business environments today.

The first driver of noise is operating with a new agile, iterative approach. Given the competitive pressures and threat of new entrants, businesses do not have the luxury of time to perfect their products and get every minute detail right. The companies that are able to grow fast and capture market share, in one way or another, experiment and pilot new products and services well before they're 100 percent ready. Google is a good example. This approach requires a lot more internal collaboration and a "launch fast, fail fast" mentality. When you pair the new approach with traditional processes, you sometimes get chaos. When a small group of people tries to deploy agile methodologies in a slow-moving, large traditional business, it results in noise.

When you're moving fast with an agile mindset, failures are also imminent. They are to be expected (discussed further in chapter 11). Launching products and services before you're fully ready will bring with them some negative feedback. The feedback loop is also a lot shorter today. People don't have the patience to see things through during times of chaos and uncertainty. Doubts are inevitable, and news spreads like wildfire, especially through an organization that has a big grapevine culture. Hence, it becomes important to block out the noise.

The second driver of noise is innovation. Many businesses are on transformational journeys. With transformation comes change—changing organizational structures, changing strategic direction, changing long-standing processes, changing areas of priority and budgets, and of course, implementing new technologies and systems. Humans hate change—that is how we're programmed. Generally we don't like when our job responsibilities change, we don't like dropping projects halfway and picking up new ones, we don't like changing our daily schedules, and we don't like switching from iPhone to Android or having to learn a brand-new system when the old one works just fine. Which means anytime there is change in the organization, there is resistance, and resistance becomes noise. For leaders and teams operating amid transformation and introducing change, blocking out the noise is a must.

As a leader, putting your headphones on allows you to operate in digital, fast-changing environments without letting it affect your performance. It keeps you focused on the long-term playbook. It allows you to stay focused on your North Star. It lets you weather the storms and see the forest from the trees. It allows you to build and operationalize teams that are focused on the things that actually matter. Your teams will stay on track. Your execution will be based on facts and data, benefiting your business and not what the squeaky wheel needs. Your teams will be happier, and morale will be higher. Net-net, putting your headphones on will allow you to make big plays in the long run despite chaos, uncertainty, and a lack of buy-in from others.

Side Note:

Everyone has an opinion, and people love giving advice on things they've never done before. I'm sure you've had your fair share of it. I have too. In high school, other players asked me why I worked so hard, because "you won't get a football scholarship" in university. Students told me that "GMAT is really hard; you won't score high enough to get accepted to an MBA program." In the MBA, classmates told me, "You don't have any experience; you won't get hired." At work, people told me to be happy with what I had, and that I was lucky to be making the salary I was for my age. The funny thing was, none of these people had actually done what they told me not to do. It's very easy to give in to these sorts of negative comments. So on a personal level, it's important to keep your headphones on and block out that negativity.

Sports to Business:

In sports, noise is everywhere. Great athletes and teams know how to put their headphones on and focus on the task at hand. Specifically, noise in the sports world includes:

1. **External Noise**

   This is the noise from everything and everyone outside the team. Media interviews, opinions, fans in the stands, newspaper articles, other teams posting on social media, and so forth. Great teams don't care about what anyone else thinks. They know all that matters is preparing and playing the game at hand.

2. **Team Noise**

   This is noise that stems from within the team. It may come from a bad locker-room presence, cliques, or groups that don't get along with others on the team, or negative sentiments toward individual players or coaches. Strong teams do a good job at minimizing this noise.

3. **Mental Noise**

   This is the noise inside the heads of athletes and coaches. It sometimes comes with negative thoughts, and sometimes it brings doubts. It also brings with itself a lack of focus and multiple distractions. For example, when an athlete misses a catch or gets disqualified for a false start, the noise gets louder.

Many athletes practice positive self-talk and visualization. Why? Because no matter who you are, mental noise is always there. But great players know how to block it out.

In business, the noise comes from lack of alignment, misunderstandings, and lack of comfort in a changing, agile, innovative environment. Noise affects the morale and energy of the team, which results in lower productivity and hampers results. Therefore, it becomes really important to block out the noise, keep yourself moving forward on your path, and focus on what really matters for your business or organization.

Here is a further breakdown of where noise originates in business today:

1. A leadership team that is changing the way they've always done things while having to maintain the interests of key stakeholders and balance sheets.
2. Peers and colleagues who are not comfortable with launching or executing in an agile and, at times, chaotic manner at fast speeds.
3. Our internal selves or our minds trying to stay focused and believe in the mission despite the chaos.

Here's a deep dive into these three levels.

Leaders: It's imperative that the leadership team sees and understands that there will be hiccups, failed projects, and bugs in launches. It's important to understand that things will not always go well in the short term. It's up to the leader of the team to overcommunicate and keep the leadership informed and ensure things are on track. There will always be questions and doubts when you do something unconventional and change an entire business model or pivot from a huge project. It's up to you, however, to ensure that the vision is communicated effectively and to influence the right people for support at the top.

Peers: Change is always hard, and as companies transform to a digital-first operating model, many of us find ourselves changing and adapting to the new approach. Changing something you've done and seen results with for many years is always tough, especially in a future filled with uncertainty. Everyone reacts differently to change, and pivots and altering processes and adding new systems will always create noise.

Our Minds: No matter how much we prepare and assure ourselves that we have a plan, and that issues are expected, doubt and negative self-talk always creep in when things get tough. It's one thing to prepare for a possible pivot or change; it's a totally different thing to actually push through one. The noise in our heads gets louder when things get tough. We start to doubt our strategy and whether the path we're on is the right one. The voices from the critics that once doubted us professionally and personally start to get louder. And this is when we need to put on those headphones and stay on course.

Action Plan:

Whether you're leading an organization-wide transformation, a new marketing launch, or trying to do the best work that you can in a noisy world, here is a five-step plan that can help you stay focused, block out the noise, and deliver results.

Step 1: Set Expectations

When you start a big project, introduce a new initiative, or implement change, it's critical to have buy-in from the key stakeholders. If you report to the CEO, then you need to be sure the CEO is 100 percent aligned with your path. At the same time, you also need to set expectations with other leaders that ultimately need to support your efforts. This will help build a solid foundation of trust and alignment before you embark on your journey, which will reduce the noise down the road.

If you're working as a one-person team, then buy into yourself. Into your vision. You need to believe that whatever path you're on is worth it, and the noise is temporary. Be honest with yourself and know that it won't be easy. In this case, you must never lose trust in your execution plan.

As a team or individual contributor, you also need to set the right expectations for milestones on your journey and not necessarily just the results. This is one of the reasons why many projects fail. Large projects and transformations take time to showcase results. If you promise just the results to your stakeholders, then all else becomes irrelevant. Instead, illustrate the key milestones that you wish to deliver on, which, when completed, will get you to your end result. For example, instead of aligning on growing digital sales by 25 percent in eighteen months, you should align on the key steps required to hit that target, such as launching new revenue channels, building a team, increasing average users on the mobile app, and so forth. Setting these expectations will minimize questions, miscommunication, and lack of trust.

Step 2: Overcommunicate

Consistent communication is a very powerful and simple, but often-overlooked skill. After setting expectations, you must keep the key stakeholders informed. When someone puts the company's balance sheet on the line for a new visionary digital product line, the last thing they want is to never hear a word about your progress.

It's imperative to communicate your progress, anticipated risks and obstacles, and changes with discretion. Most of the noise will be eliminated if you keep the key folks updated with conviction. Nothing should ever be a surprise, and laying out a contingency plan ahead of time and communicating it with the leadership team will help reduce this noise. Let everyone know that there will be issues in production, and that you'll get some angry customers. This is why chapter 2 is so important—building your playbook while anticipating future needs will help you reduce the noise down the road. Once that is done, you need to continue communicating your progress.

The same goes for broader teams. Overcommunicate your vision. If you're bringing change, let everyone know that it's going to be messy, and it won't be all fun. Keeping the teams informed and updated will help answer questions before they arise, which then keeps the noise down. If you didn't hear about a big change coming to your department that would affect you personally, there's a very high likelihood that you would be asking your peers and colleagues a ton of questions. So overcommunicate your plans and progress. Reduce the noise up front.

I had a simple rule in my team: two emails and a phone call. If you send someone an email and there are more than two replies, and the problem isn't solved, pick up the phone. No more back and forth after two email responses. The third time an email comes back, you call the other person. It's simple stuff that saves everyone a lot of trouble. And most of the time things got sorted out over one phone call. We saved time this way and actually strengthened our relationships with other teams.

Step 3: Facts and Data-Based Execution

During the Q&A portion of one of my keynotes, an audience member asked, "How do you keep your team motivated when you know there will be issues, and everyone is breathing down your neck?" A problem that she was dealing with at the time. My answer was simple: execute with data and facts, not emotions.

Aligning expectations and communicating will reduce noise, but some noise will always find a way to trickle through to you and your team. When you're executing, you block out the noise by operating based on facts and data. Every team should have targets that are quantifiable and measurable. For example, teams should be working toward specific deliverables such as launching a tech product in a certain number of retail locations, filing a certain number of new patents, completing specific project deliverables, or growing sales by a certain percentage. When you're working toward specific goals and outcomes, the issues and noise merely become a part of execution. Oftentimes, we lose sight of the key reasons why we're doing something, and that's when we get sidetracked. Therefore, always drive your team with facts and data-first milestones.

When things go sideways, teams need to execute according to plan and stay the course. There's no reason to get caught up in what others think, feel, or say. If you find your team getting more worried about what others think or starting to lose motivation in situations like these, then you need to get the team to focus back on the key deliverables. Show them what actually matters and what to focus on. Data, facts, and clear objectives become your noise-canceling headphones.

At a personal level, the same idea applies. You can block the noise out by focusing on areas that are backed by data and facts. If you find yourself stuck and you feel that everyone's eyes are on you and emotions are running high, just take a step back. Ask yourself what you can do today, tomorrow, or this month, objectively, to get out of this hole. Once you figure out what you need to do, then execute.

Step 4: Shelter Your Team

Good leaders lead. Great leaders lead, empower, and influence. It's solely a leader's responsibility to ensure their team is free of major distractions and doesn't get caught up in any negative backlash from external sources and partner teams. Ensure that you keep the team focused on the road ahead and clear the path.

The slightest noise, such as a possible change in direction, someone's opinion of the team's recent project, or anything minute can have a large, detrimental impact on your team's productivity. A leader cannot expect their team to hear everything directly from the source and take it without any impact. That is why the team has a leader. The leader needs to then determine what to communicate to the team, how to communicate it, and, at times, to wait for the right moment.

Remember that your key objective is to deliver whatever you're working on, so keep your team focused and be that filter.

Stage 5: Remember Why You Started

Lastly, when things get really loud, never forget why you started. These are the moments that will make or break your performance. At times you may feel that everyone is against you. You may feel that you're being singled out in meetings. You may feel that no one believes you can do it. You may even feel that you bit off more than you could chew.

You need to always remember why you took on this role, responsibility, challenge, or endeavor. There was a reason. Find it and keep it in front of you. It will help you block out the noise. You need to be able to clearly see your vision and finish line.

Also, don't worry about "what if." Yes, there might be a chance that you may fail or that you might not succeed at bringing the change you had promised. But it's better to focus on your vision and execute versus standing still and giving up without a fight. When the noise gets loud, remember your "why," put on your headphones, and get to work.

Side Note:

I called a team meeting one day, while we were getting ripped apart for a recent launch that did not go as planned. I simply reminded the team that there was a reason why we had all decided to take this project on. It was a lot bigger than whatever was going on. I said, "At this moment, it seems really bad, and all eyes are on us. But once we're through this, none of this will matter. All you're going to remember is the results that you delivered and the impact you made." We kept marching forward as planned and delivered the project successfully. It was a big win for the team.

When I look back, there are also other times when I wish I had just continued on with the execution, and the results would have spoken for themselves. Such situations are all about hunkering down and believing in the path you chose. Change always comes with resistance.

Exercise:

- When projects or product launches are met with bumps along the road, how does your leadership team react? What can you do to make it smoother? (Hint: overcommunicate.)

  ____

  ____

  ____

- Think about your current projects. What are a few ways you can keep your team executing on the set path when things go sideways? How can you block out the noise?

  ____

  ____

  ____

CHAPTER 7

Get Your Game Face On

Get in the Zone

Our defense had gathered for our weekly meeting the day before a playoff game during the 2012 season. We were going to play in the national semifinal game and had a chance to make history by winning a bowl game at home, and competing for the national title for the second year in a row. It was a big deal. In the meeting, we were watching game film with our defensive coordinator Greg Knox, a former CFL player and two-time Grey Cup champion.

An hour-and-a-half later, after we had exhausted the game film, Coach Knox exited the game tape and went on YouTube. He turned off the lights and played a video called *Brian Dawkins History-Weapon X*. Brian Dawkins is a former NFL football safety who played sixteen seasons in the NFL. He played the majority of his career for the Philadelphia Eagles. He is a nine-time Pro Bowl selection, four-time first team All-Pro and NFL 2000s

All-Decade team. In other words, he is one of the most successful football safeties to have ever played the game. This video was about Brian Dawkins's alter ego, the Weapon X, a character from the X-Men comics and movies, and also known as the Wolverine.

In this ten-minute video, Brian Dawkins explains his fascination with Wolverine. He shows his two different lockers in the Eagles locker room, one with a name plate reading Brian Dawkins and the other that reads *Weapon X, Wolverine*. The video also shows Brian Dawkins's pregame rituals, where he spends time transforming into the Wolverine. Some of the clips show him pacing around the field, crawling out of the tunnel, and talking to the football in the end zone. He attributes his success on the field to this alter ego, which allowed him to get into a state of mind where he was able to push himself further than he otherwise could.

As we watched the video, I remember the energy in our locker room changing. It was well timed by Coach Knox. After preparing all week long, he saw that what we needed was some fire. We needed to get our game faces on. The Wolverine was Brian Dawkins's way of getting his game face on. It was his way of getting ready before the game and getting fully dialed in for whatever was going to come his way. Sharing Dawkins's prep was coach Knox's attempt to get us ready to get in the zone for one of the biggest games of our college football careers.

Coach Knox followed the video with a pregame talk. I remember when we left the locker room that night, it was very quiet. The quietest I had ever seen our defense the day before a game. But this was a good quiet. The quiet you hear right before a big storm. We were focused. We were ready to get our game faces on.

The next day we beat the University of Calgary football team 45–6. We made our way back to the Vanier Cup—where we faced the Laval Rouge et Or again at the Rogers Centre in Toronto in front of over thirty-seven thousand fans.

Concept:

In order to execute in the face of challenges, obstacles, change, and uncertainty, you need to get in the right state of mind. Game face is our ability to switch from a relaxed, "everyday" state to a hyper-focused state and become fixated on the task at hand. It's about proactively and mentally preparing for what's to come and bringing a sense of urgency in an environment that is fast and chaotic.

It also means taking ownership of the hand that is dealt to us with pride, and doing the best we can with what we have. There are things you can't control, such as what others think about you, office politics, or bad weather before an important meeting. But how you respond and react to circumstances outside your control is what defines great leaders.

It's about not letting the magnitude or pressure of the task ahead impact your confidence. It's about having a process where we know exactly what is required of us to get the job done. And it's about putting aside our differences or bitterness toward our teammates and having each other's backs and everyone's best interest in mind.

In other words, game face is an attitude.

Game face is super important in the times we're operating in. It is one of the best ways to combat chaos and uncertainty in a high-pressure situation. There are two recent drivers that make it critical for leaders and teams to be able to tap into their hyper-focused states.

First, the amount and magnitude of high-pressure, "firefighting" situations are increasing. Disruption comes with a higher number of iterations and directional changes, which raises the volume and the importance of daily actions. Reacting to consumer feedback on a new app, responding to a competitor's limited time offer, or addressing a regulation that affects your store operations all come with high-pressure, high-stakes execution. While we work on better predicting these pivotal situations by investing in the right foundations and a long-term plan, this is a reality most teams need to deal with.

Second, we're living in a world of constant change with work that is becoming unpredictable. As we've discussed throughout the book, the new normal is constant transformation and adjustments to better meet rising consumer demands and advances in technology. With the need to constantly change, comes uncertainty and periods of unpredictability. Long-standing three-to-five-year roadmaps no longer work. Think about the last time you planned a two-week vacation months in advance, thinking it's going to be a slow time at work, only to realize you may have to reschedule as you got closer to the date. Given the constant change and uncertainty, work and execution will happen more and more as sprints and in waves, and these waves will be somewhat unpredictable.

These two drivers make it crucial for us to discover, practice, and hone the ability to flick that switch that puts us in the right state of the mind—we need to learn how to get that game face on. It's important to have a certain trigger that gives us the ability to focus and execute on that last-minute project, troubleshoot a company-wide issue, not check our mobile phone every fifteen minutes, or to not let competitor news alter our execution for the day. Getting your game face on will help you handle high-pressure, high-stakes initiatives and tasks and deliver on last-minute projects and business needs without feeling overwhelmed. You'll always be ready to take on whatever comes your way. You'll feel more in control, and things will feel less chaotic. Getting your game face on will let you make big plays during moments that matter the most.

Side Note:

When I was working as a product manager, I received a call from a teammate while driving to work one morning. He said, "Hey, the app is down." It was seven thirty in the morning, and we had an app outage that affected over a million users. This was going to be a disaster. I said, "OK, I'll see you in ten. Get ready." I knew it was going to be a tough morning. We would need to get all four external vendor partners on a call and troubleshoot the issue before lunch time, while managing expectations with leadership. There was also the possibility of making some customers really angry.

I knew I needed to get my mind right before I got to the office. I had a playlist I used specifically for working out. It was designed to get me focused and get some adrenaline pumping. So I cranked up the volume and played my "pump-up songs" playlist in the car. As I got to the parking lot, I was calm but ready for whatever came our way. Similar to how I felt leaving the locker room after Coach Knox showed us the video, I had my game face on. Looking back at the day, had I not prepared myself mentally beforehand, it would not have been a story I would want to remember.

Sports to Business:

Across sports, many great players are known to get "in the zone" and get their game faces on. Ray Lewis, Serena Williams, Cristiano Ronaldo, Usain Bolt, LeBron James. When you see them play on TV, you can see nothing but focus and confidence in their eyes. These players have a very different personality when they're in the middle of a game than when they're at home with their families. At home, superstar athletes are just like everyone else. They relax, have fun, watch Netflix, go on dates with their significant others, and organize their son or daughter's birthday parties.

But before a competition, these same athletes have a switch that they can flick. Flicking the switch allows them to focus with conviction. It allows them to block out all that is going on in their personal lives and be present in the moment. It allows them to dial up the intensity that is needed to compete against other elite athletes in high-pressure situations. It allows them to turn on the hunt mentality as if their lives depend on it. It allows them to put on a performance that is perhaps the best one yet because that is the level of play that is needed if they are to win.

Specifically, game face in sports applies at the following levels:

1. **Individual Athlete Level**
   This is an athlete's ability to turn their game face on during practice and competition. There's a lot of prep work that goes into performing at a peak level. There are workout sessions in the gym or on the track, there are film study sessions, there are practices, and there are walk-throughs and mental prep sessions. All of these require 100 percent focus and attention. Why? Because any elite athlete will tell you that the intensity you practice at is the intensity you will play at. No one can ever practice and work out at 50 percent intensity and expect to somehow turn it up to 100 percent in the game.

   Therefore, great athletes practice and prepare at a level of intensity, focus, and determination that is close to the real game. It might not always be at 100 percent, but they do enter that zone from time to time during preparation.

And when it's actually time to compete, the game face simply becomes a flick of the switch.

2. **Team Level**

   There's something to be said about the collective momentum of a team. Having a few players with their game faces on will do no good if the remainder of the team is not ready to compete at the level required to win. Therefore, teams that win have the ability to get their game face on as a team. Everyone raises their level of intensity.

   A great strategy that most coaches utilize is counting on a few select teammates to get the rest of the team in the zone. Coaches will have their go-to players for when it's time to get the team ready before a big game, a hard workout, or even throughout a game where the team needs a jolt of energy.

   In a business environment filled with data overload, speed, and uncertainty, leaders cannot be expected to lead teams and make the right decisions without the right mindset. It's important to get into the right state of mind before any big presentation, event, or big performance.

The game face concept helps with this on a few specific occasions:

1. **Unexpected Fires**

   When things break and every minute that goes by results in a loss of revenue for the business. It becomes super important for the individual or team fixing the issue to operate with a sense of urgency, an aligned objective, and focus. The game face helps bring that sense of urgency and focus in such situations.

2. **High-Stakes Event or Presentation**
   There are times when there's a high-stakes speech to an executive board, for example, or a presentation where you're asking people to change the company's direction, or a proposal where you're asking for more money. During these moments, it's important to be confident and at peak performance. The game face helps get people ready to fire on all cylinders.

   During these critical moments, sometimes things may also take a wrong turn—things one can't control. Game face is a must in order to hunker down and give it your best regardless of the circumstances.

3. **Final Stages of a Project or Initiative**
   Most projects have a final push, whether it's launching a physical product, implementing software solutions, unveiling a new virtual reality product, or a new marketing campaign. Each of these milestones come with high pressure, as it's the first time where it will be launched at scale, will be shown to the leadership team, or will gather real feedback. Therefore, it becomes important to anticipate and tackle any challenges that may arise

during go time. Great leaders get themselves ready to rock and roll and deal with things as they come their way.

Action Plan:

Here is an action plan to help you get your game face on when you need it the most.

Step 1: Identify Three Upcoming Mission-Critical Performances

Being intense every day, all the time, is never a good idea. It's tough to sustain high levels of intensity 24-7. It can also lead to burnout. Therefore, identify the scenarios, projects, deliverables, situations, or events that require a heightened level of focus and energy from your team. These can be quarterly presentations to the board, for example. Or it can be your upcoming product launches or your monthly team meeting. If you have an unpredictable role, then identify possible scenarios where you may have to react with full focus, such as dealing with an issue on the weekend that affects more than 20 percent of your customers. Whatever it is, identify it clearly.

As an individual, list your personal upcoming performances. A leader needs to prepare to get their own game face on before they can get the team ready to execute. Write down the most critical preplanned performances that you personally need to be 100 percent present for.

Step 2: Build an Individual Game Plan

Now, you might already have something that gets you in the zone when things are on the line, such as meditating, reading motivational quotes, calling a friend, or an inspirational scene from your favourite movie. Or this might be something you haven't given much thought to. But everyone has something that gets us ready to take on that big challenge. The key is to identify one to two inputs that allow you to tap into the "ready to take on the world" feeling.

If you think you have a good idea of what's worked in the past, then think back to when you performed at peak capacity and see if this was indeed one of the inputs. Recall the last time you were "in the zone." What did it feel like? Was it during a big presentation or during an interview? Or was it when you were asked to step up and deliver under pressure? Or was it during your weekend ten-kilometer run, and you hit a personal best? Try and remember what it felt like to be in the zone. The idea here is to find out the stimulus behind that state so that you can start to replicate it when you need it.

If you're not sure what helps you, then you can start by looking back at a time when you did your best work. For example, maybe you spent ten to fifteen minutes alone before the presentation that you knocked out of the park last month. What was it about that project, that presentation, or that problem you solved that allowed you to perform at your best? What did you do just before? Did you go for a workout in the morning, did you speak to a friend who always helps you see the positive side of things, or did you simply have a good night's sleep? Find out what might be the inputs that helped you perform at your peak.

If you're struggling to think of what helped you get in the zone, then think about a time when you failed at a task or were sent into an uncontrolled panic state. What factors might have caused you to spiral out of control? If you notice a pattern, you should build a system to avoid those influences in the future.

Once you have your inputs, then find a way to make it repeatable on demand. For example, if you feel music is what gets you going, then make a playlist on Spotify or YouTube that you can access when you need it. If you get your game face on after a pep talk from your best friend, then tell your friend you may need her help. Give her a heads-up anytime you can anticipate the future.

Step 3: Build Team Game Plan

Once you've figured out how to get yourself in the zone, now you need to get your team ready.

Look back at your team's performance. What gets your team pumped up? When do they do their best work? For example, do office-wide town hall meetings get them in the zone? Does a small weekly huddle get them ready? Does a surprise pep talk from the CEO get the team fired up? See what has worked in the past.

Also identify who are your go-to team members who will energize and pick up the team intensity when it's time to execute. Take a look at who provides the energy for your team. Who are those one or two individuals who usually set the tone, make decisions, and are genuine leaders? These are the ones you're going to need to call on to get the team in the zone when the time comes. Similar to step 2, write these down and find a way to make them repeatable.

Step 4: Practice with Your Game Face On

Practice makes perfect. Once you identify the scenarios and concrete steps to getting yourself and your team in the zone, now it's about finding ways to practice "flicking the switch" in a situation as close as it can get to real life.

This practice needs to occur at two levels: individual and team.

Individual: Identify upcoming opportunities where you can practice executing with a sense of urgency and focus. It could be an upcoming presentation or an interim milestone. The act of preparing and getting in the right state of mind is more important than the magnitude of the event. The goal is to practice getting your game face on so you know how it feels, and then getting enough reps for you to become comfortable to simply flick the switch in the future.

Team: Similarly, take inventory of your upcoming milestones and deliverables as a team and identify where you can get in some good reps. Think of it as an exhibition or a preseason match where you're playing at a high intensity, but the game doesn't count toward the standings. For example, you can do a mock troubleshooting session or treat a small pilot launch as the big thing. It's important to communicate the expectations and value behind this exercise to your team and ensure they understand the why.

Exercise:

- What are some rituals or routines that help you get in the zone before a big event? For example, do you find some quiet time alone before a big presentation? How can you make them repeatable on demand?

  ____

  ____

  ____

- How do you prepare to take on the day? Do you meditate? List the things that you do to help you get in the zone on a daily basis. How can you do them more consistently?

  ____

  ____

  ____

- What is your team's energy like during a big kickoff or a big day? What are some things that you can do to elevate your team's energy, if it is not at the level where you want it to be?

  ____

  ____

  ____

CHAPTER 8

Keep Your Eyes on the Prize—80/20 Rule

Do a Few Things, but Do Them Really Well

In high school, I had pretty much taught myself how to work out and train. I read a lot of articles, watched plenty of videos, and tried to incorporate all interesting elements into my workout. So at one point in grade twelve, my workout program included exercises from a bodyweight training program I'd seen at school, some exercises from a Julius Peppers video, a few lifts from famous bodybuilders, and then some exercises that my friends and I thought made sense.

To have enough time for all this, I was working out every single day, twice a day. I thought more time would allow me to train different muscle groups more frequently. I was also working out for two to three hours at a time. I felt very proud of my routine!

The following year in the summer of 2008, I started attending the off-season workouts at McMaster University leading up to my first training camp. To my surprise and shock, these workouts were very...simple.

I was quite confused. These workouts didn't include any of the fancy stuff I was doing. They were hard, no doubt, but simple. When I finally received my first in-season workout program during training camp, it was again a very basic program. It included a few major lifts three times a week and was only meant to last forty-five minutes. There were just a handful of major movements such as the bench press, squats, and deadlifts, with a lot of flexibility and stretching. I was skeptical. How could I get stronger and bigger while working out for only forty-five minutes a day? And only three times a week? It didn't make sense.

So I looked forward to the full team practice instead, excited to learn some new fancy moves. The practice turned out to be longer, faster, and higher tempo but nothing that I hadn't seen before. The drills we did as defensive linemen revolved around just a handful of schemes like becoming strong run stoppers. Things we had learned in high school. And things every other team did around the league.

But the difference here was that the coaching staff really focused on our technique through repetition. We repped the same things again and again, every practice. Even as the season progressed, we saw the same formula applied to the playbook schemes and formations. We repped the same schemes and formations day in and day out.

By November 2008, my perspective had started to shift. Having gone through my first full season as a college football player, I realized that these simple workouts were actually effective. The practices weren't fancy, but I got better as a lineman week over week. The playbook didn't change much except for a few weekly adjustments, but our execution of those plays got much better as the week went on.

What really made the difference for me was when I injured my shoulder during a workout heading into the holidays. I realized how harmful my high-school workouts were. The injury assessment concluded that I had developed imbalances in my upper body from the training I did back in high school. I had a weaker back and rear shoulders compared to my chest. It wasn't something I had prioritized, as I was training for the sake of training, and not training to be a better defensive lineman.

It was during those holidays that I had an "aha" moment where it all started to make sense. My workouts in high school were not aligned with my goals. The McMaster program was. The in-season workout program was designed to keep us healthy and maintain our strength, not to bulk up. The practice drills focused on getting our young defensive line to learn strong fundamentals like stopping the running plays. If a defense could not stop the run, nothing else would matter. The offense would simply keep running the ball, which eats up time on the clock and tires out the defense.

So the ultimate goal was to win games, keep the players healthy, and build the foundations for years to come. And the training sessions, practices, and playbook were all designed to take us closer to that goal.

This brings us to the concept known as keeping your eyes on the prize.

Concept:

To execute your strategy effectively, you need to make sure that you're working on the things that actually matter. Keeping your eyes on the prize means to always focus on your top-level goal by picking a handful of priorities and tasks that get you to that goal or destination. The 80/20 rule (a.k.a. The Pareto Principle) is a big proponent of this concept. All of us are solving problems or making decisions on a regular basis, and the 80/20 rule allows you to identify the key drivers of the desired objective. It helps you pick the 20 percent of the most important actions. It is designed to make you only focus on the few things that have the maximum impact on your objectives.

As discussed in this book, there are a plethora of options and solutions available to leaders today in the form of technologies, decisions, business strategies, etc. Data bombardment is real, and there is seldom ever a clear path in the middle of a muddy fight. When you focus on too many goals or objectives and don't have a clear path to hitting those objectives, the performance of the entire organization suffers. You become less efficient, your actions don't always lead to the results you need, and productivity takes a hit.

Furthermore, one cannot expect a leader, an individual, or a team to deliver on ten competing priorities with perfection, even with unlimited resources. As humans, we can only focus on three to four highly critical priorities or initiatives if we're looking to maximize success.

Therefore, it becomes critical to pick a few priorities and break them down into smaller chunks, which can then be assigned as projects or initiatives to your teams. Once you've identified the top three to four overarching organization or team-wide goals, then you need to identify the actions to get you there. These sub-actions can be in the form of projects, new products, or process improvements and can continue to be further broken down into smaller chunks, depending on the levels in a company's hierarchy and the number of employees.

This is where the 80/20 rule comes into play. It is important to identify your objective, and then distill down the 20 percent of the actions that you need to take to get you 80 percent of the way there. Take the example of a business trying to grow sales. There are hundreds of options available to the business. But it's critical to first quantify the objective.

In this example, let us say the goal from the CEO is to grow sales by 15 percent over the year. Then we need to identify the key drivers of this 15 percent growth, which could include (1) increasing existing revenue streams or (2) finding new revenue streams. If we focus on existing revenue streams, we can either (1) sell more to existing customers, (2) find new customers, or (3) increase the price. If we focus on increasing price, this may mean adding new product features, having a tiered pricing structure, or upping our brand positioning.

You would continue to dig deeper in this decision tree for three to four levels. At the end you would pick the top 20 percent of actions that would help find an additional 15 percent in sales. In this example, the final three to four actions will become the only thing the team or employee will focus on for the next six to twelve months. It works because these 20 percent of the actions will directly drive your top-line goals.

The 80/20 rule will also help you decide between competing priorities. For example, maybe you're leading the marketing or strategy for a retail chain and have just been tasked with finding new revenue streams. You realize that the team is currently maxed out in capacity and doesn't have room to take on more. Usually our gut instinct will tell us that we need to hire more people, or we don't have the capacity to do this. But this is the beauty of the 80/20 rule. In addition to prioritizing new initiatives to tackle, it can be used to reevaluate existing tasks so as to potentially discontinue low-value work in favor of higher-impact activities.

If you apply the 80/20 rule in the example above, then the first thing you should do is to take an inventory of all the projects and tasks the team is working on today. You should identify which of these projects are helping you find new revenue streams. Through this exercise, there's a high likelihood that you may find some projects that are not helping with your new goals. This may result in pausing and discontinuing some projects that are no longer relevant, or combining and realigning efforts to help save time and resources. In both cases, you can achieve your goals with no additional head count by focusing on the 20 percent of the options that actually matter.

Sports to Business:

When we look at the world of sports, great teams, regardless of the league or level, always keep their eyes on the prize. A team may lose a game or two, but it does not derail them from their goal. Why? Because they operate with the understanding that as long as they do the key things day in and day out, they will continue to improve. Over the course of the year or multiple seasons, they will get closer to the championship. They understand it's a continuous battle and one that must be won with consistency.

This means focusing on a few critical priorities day in and day out during the season, such as the following:

- Practicing with intensity
- Investing time studying the opponent's game film
- Being committed to recovery sessions after each workout
- Instilling belief and positivity as a coaching staff
- Spending time with your team off the field to strengthen the on-field chemistry

In business this translates to first identifying your top two or three objectives for the year in a specific and quantifiable manner, and then prioritizing the 20 percent of activities that will get you there.

1. **Identify the top three priorities**
   The analysis begins with leadership's top three priorities. This generally includes goals tied to the operating model, such as increasing profitability, gaining market share, improving workplace culture, and so on.

2. **Drill down**
   This is where you drill into the top priorities that allow the company as a whole to meet the top-level goals. The exercise includes identifying key drivers for each objective and repeating the process until you get three to four levels deep. At the end, there is a comprehensive list of actions that can be taken to achieve the top priorities.

3. **Select the 20 percent**
   These are actions (drivers) that have the highest return on your time and effort, similar to the priorities above for a sports team. So a leader must pick the 20 percent that will provide the highest ROIt.

   In this case, for example, if the goal is to increase revenues by $1 million, then the following priorities may constitute the 20 percent:

   - Increasing brand awareness through digital channels
   - Launching four new campaigns bolstering an existing product line

- Building and launching a new direct-to-consumer channel

All three objectives help with the overarching goal of gaining revenue. These actions are then assigned to teams and individuals depending on the size and depth of your company. These actions are further broken down into action plans, which is discussed in chapter 9.

Action Plan:

How can you keep your eyes on the prize? Here is a four-step action plan.

Step 1: Communicate the Vision—The Why

How many times have we heard someone say, "My team isn't performing well. My team's focusing on the wrong things"? Or "They just don't get it." Well, if a team doesn't understand the vision and where you're going, how can it possibly build a plan of attack with no clear destination?

Have your team understand what the business goals are and, more importantly, why these are the goals (from chapters 1 and 2). Be as clear and articulate as you can be. It's always a good idea to have your top three goals and objectives for the year front and center. You could print them out and stick them to your wall, add them to your desktop background, or open every team meeting by repeating these objectives. Everyone needs to have the same understanding of where you are headed and what you're trying to achieve. The same applies at the individual level. You need to know where you're headed, especially during the tough times.

Side Note:

One of our clients wasn't very happy with the performance of a particular star player and asked us to help. The employee wasn't responding well to the internal changes at the company and kept working on things that weren't high priority. I asked the client, "When was the last time you communicated your expectations of their role and your definition of success?"

The client responded, "Over a year ago" (when the business was in a much different place). Realizing why I asked that question, the client scheduled a one-to-one meeting with the employee the same week. They aligned on the priorities, what success looked like amid all the change and chaos, and the "why" behind some of the tasks. Within just a few weeks, the star player's performance dramatically improved. All it took was one meeting with clear communication and alignment on the vision.

Step 2: Break Down the Plays

Identify the 20 percent of the priorities you and the team need to tackle in order to achieve your overarching objectives and to ensure everyone in your organization is driving toward these objectives. Numerous studies suggest that we are programmed to remember and recall information in chunks of three. Therefore, if you have a list of ten potential priorities or ten different actions that you believe will help you drive profitability, then focus on the three that provide the highest ROI.

Every individual in your organization must have a clear understanding of their own 20 percent. Whether it's the CEO or a summer intern, everyone should be able to clearly state the three to four priorities that they need to deliver on for the year. The goal here is to make sure that everyone in your organization or your project team, including yourself, has a clear understanding of their priorities. And the priorities need to be directly tied to the goals from step 1. Even if you're a part of the special projects team or innovation lab, the actions still need to tie into the overall goals of the company.

Once you identify these key actions, then it comes down to communicating to the team why these are the most important actions. This would include illustrating how the smaller actions and projects will help the overall business objective—think of it like positive visualization into the future.

Step 3: Build Checkpoints

As a leader, set up weekly and/or monthly status meetings. Review the projects the team is working on and have the team present them to you with what the milestones are, what they worked on, and what is coming up. This will allow you to see whether the team is focused on the key results, and it's also a great time to coach and realign focus. At every checkpoint ask whether the actions and subprojects are in fact the 20 percent to help you achieve 80 percent of your goal. Identify whether these are the best 20 percent that you should be focusing on.

At an individual level, a common blind spot that we need to be aware of is doing work that doesn't get us to our goal. Every day, we do many things that are a waste of time or energy. We do them either because we think we're being productive by doing work or because it's part of a process that is no longer relevant. At times it's because we personally feel good about doing a certain task or project, or it has emotional value. Perhaps you've been doing certain things as a team for so long that you never stopped to think whether they're still adding value.

It's really hard to constantly evaluate whether or not what we're doing is adding the most value. Weekly or monthly checkpoints allow you to take a step back from the nitty gritty details and focus on the big picture. Therefore, build personal checkpoints on a weekly or monthly basis to evaluate your own 20 percent. It will help you remove inefficiencies and streamline your personal execution. I usually spend some time on Sunday mornings for my personal checkpoints. That's when I feel the most removed from the day to day.

Step 4: Readjust

As things change constantly in today's digital-first world, the key priorities identified six months ago may no longer be relevant.

Take a step back every six months and see whether your overarching objectives are still the same or if they need to be changed. For example, it may be easier to enter a new market today versus six months ago due to a recently introduced regulation. Or a tech giant just unveiled its plans to launch a product that will go head-to-head with one of your product lines. These were not a part of your strategic plan six months ago but now pose new challenges or opportunities. Therefore, readjust the top-level priorities every six months or as needed.

Determine how changes in priorities change your goals and what actions need to be readjusted. Then simply drill down to the 20 percent required to achieve these new objectives and communicate the vision and the plays to the team. This is a continuous process and one that has to be repeated consistently.

Side Note:

After my football career was over, I cut down a significant amount of weight. It helped me alleviate lingering issues from previous injuries. I was pain-free for the first few years, but I had also lost some strength. In an effort to regain strength and become my strongest self at this new weight, I decided to reestablish parts of my football workouts. I started lifting heavy weights again—heavy squats, deadlifts, and Olympic lifting. It felt great, and I loved it!

But with time, my left knee started to bother me again (I had previously injured it during football). I didn't think much of it and kept working out. Shortly after, I developed imbalances in my body and hurt my lower back during heavy deadlifts. I regularly visited physiotherapists and practitioners, who recommended focusing on mobility and flexibility. I added these to my program, but it didn't help much. I kept working out, and the downward spiral continued.

Finally, during a visit to McMaster University in late 2021, I ran into Chris Puskas, our football head athletic therapist. Chris was kind enough to help me get to the bottom of these injuries. He had treated me for my knee and shoulder injuries during my football years, so I trusted his judgment. He asked me if I had been working out. I told him about the types of exercises and the heavy weights that I had been lifting.

He smiled and asked, "Tanvir, what are you training for?" And that's when the light bulb went off in my head. There was no reason for me to be lifting such heavy weights, given I was not playing football anymore. I realized my actions weren't aligned to my priorities. I immediately changed my workout plan, removed the heavy and high-impact exercises, and focused on mobility, flexibility, and suppleness. Within a few weeks, I was pain-free.

Exercise:

Answer the following questions to see whether you keep your eyes on the prize:

Individual standpoint:

- What are your top-level goals? Do they stem from the goals of your leadership team or CEO?

  ____

  ____

  ____

- Evaluate whether the 20 percent of activities you're working on is going to get you 80 percent of the way there. Are you focusing on the right priorities?

  ____

  ____

  ____

- Look at the past four weeks and analyze the meetings in your calendar, your to-do lists, and other work you did. Was everything that you worked on directly aligned to your top-level goals?

  ____

  ____

  ____

Team standpoint:

- Do a tally of all the projects and subtasks for each project or initiative. How many of these are truly adding value to the organization's top-level goals?

  ___

  ___

  ___

- Analyze a past decision or project where your team pulled together tons of reports and analysis. What information actually made a difference, and what didn't add any value? What can you do differently next time?

  ___

  ___

  ___

CHAPTER 9

Game of Inches

Show Up Every Single Day

In early November 2015, my parents surprised me with tickets to a Hamilton Tiger-Cats Football Game (CFL). We showed up a little early to the brand-new Tim Hortons Field, while the players were still warming up. As fans slowly started filling up the stands, we bought our Tim Hortons coffees and made our way to our seats.

For weeks leading up to the game, I had been feeling a little sloppy. I was going through a bit of a rough patch. My dedication, drive, and mindset were not where I wanted them to be. I was finding it hard to commit to a decision and execute.

Back at the stadium, some of the players were on the field going through their own pregame rituals and routines prior to the team warm-ups. These individual warm-ups or drills included getting some mental reps, injury prevention work, or getting some quiet time to get in the zone (chapter 7).

One player in particular caught my attention, a defensive back for the Tiger-Cats. He was warming up on the sidelines closer to us, wearing a black and yellow jersey, nicely tucked in. He stood out from the rest of his team with yellow arm bands to match the jersey, bright yellow gloves, and a shiny black helmet with a black tinted visor.

Something seemed different about this player's whole routine. There was a certain positivity to it. I wasn't sure what it was, but something made me happy to just watch. He started every drill on the goal line and ended at the fifteen-yard line. Every single rep, including his last rep, started exactly on the goal line and finished only when he crossed the fifteen-yard line. Not an inch before. Every rep of every drill was consistent, with equal intensity.

At the end of his routine, he took his helmet off at the five-yard line, jogged over to the end zone, took a knee, and prayed. Then he got up again, pointed to the sky, and sprinted back to the five-yard line. At that point, it hit me: this man was on a mission! He was meticulous. He was precise. He exuded confidence. He knew what was expected of him, and he welcomed the opportunity to put in the work. He was only focused on the task at hand. Zero distractions. He was playing for the love of the game. He was playing to prove something. He was playing for something greater than a paycheck.

I don't remember the final score, but I took away a few things that day. First, this player was putting himself in the best possible position to make plays. It was clear that he believed how well he performed in this game was directly proportional to how well he prepared. Second, this routine was not something he made up on the spot. He had been doing this for years. Whatever his career goals were, he had planned for, practiced, and executed this core element consistently. Lastly, he was a veteran, yet he prepared as if someone was watching his every move and evaluating him. He didn't think he was above putting in the work.

This was an awakening. I could not expect results if I wasn't willing to commit and execute consistently and stay the course. The work you put in, day in and day out, is what defines success. It reminded me that I have a long way to go, and no matter what I accomplish, I'll always need to consistently build my foundations and execute like my life depends on it.

I left the stadium feeling motivated and encouraged. The crappy feeling I had brought with me to the game was gone. If one of the best players on the field, who had nothing to prove, played like it was his first professional game, then I had no excuse. Executing with diligence and staying the course became my mantra to succeed.

Concept:

In addition to focusing on the right things, you need to be consistent in doing whatever gets you closer to your goals. The game of inches requires consistent execution. It entails performing the tasks, actions, and processes designed to take us closer to the finish line. Executing day in and day out without deviating from the plan. The key here is consistency.

The game of inches is about focusing on the small steps that bring us closer to the big goals. It's about building the routines and mindsets that help us focus on what we can do today, versus worrying about getting to our final destination.

Consistent execution doesn't necessarily mean we never change our strategy or find a better way of doing things. It merely means that whatever path we choose, along with the right contingency plans, we must execute on that path consistently with full focus and determination. Consistent execution is about showing up to work every single day and doing your best regardless of the situation. It is about not letting one bad day stop you from executing the next day.

In team environments, this concept of showing up every day is even more critical. If one person misses their assignment or isn't detail oriented, or if something slips through the cracks, it could negatively impact the outcome of an entire initiative. All it takes is someone taking one play off. For better or for worse, team consistency is a product of individual consistency. If an integral team member doesn't embrace their role fully, will you be able to become the best team out there? Most of the time, the answer is an unfortunate no.

At an individual level, performing to the best of your abilities day in and day out will always outperform spurts in performance in the long run. You need to do your best work every single day. That is what moves things along. When your team is counting on you, it's about doing the best you can with what you have.

One of the biggest reasons why great strategies fail is poor execution. Strategies always look good on paper, just like a football play drawn up on a whiteboard with complex routes and twists. But not every team can execute it to perfection. Nowadays, with the internet, it's easier to uncover your competition's strategy. You can easily research what investments someone is making, whom they've hired, what technologies they've acquired, etc. But what sets great leaders, businesses, and organizations apart from mediocre ones is execution. The leader who identifies the actions that need to be performed daily and stays the course will outperform the leader with a groundbreaking strategy but inconsistent execution. It's about showing up, every single day, and putting in the work.

There are a few key factors that make up great execution.

First is breaking down the daunting goals into digestible chunks. It's hard to make progress on something that seems big and scary. It's even more challenging when you add in a disruptive environment with tight timelines, resource constraints, and no clear path to success. When this happens, you start hearing things like, "The timelines are super tight...there's no way this is going to happen...this isn't feasible in the time we have...this is impossible."

This is avoidable by taking the time up front to break down the goals into action plans and gain team alignment.

Second, it's imperative to focus on the right things. When things get hard or we feel under pressure, we develop tunnel vision, tend to think less creatively, and lose perspective on what is truly important (covered in detail in chapter 8). As a result you either start doing things that don't add value or you start to worry. Both of these are culprits in bad execution. Instead, what you need are systems, processes, and routines that allow you to focus objectively on the tasks and execute.

Third, you need to be committed to the selected path. The amount of options and solutions being thrown at leaders today is only increasing. Every week someone sends me an email about a new solution, tech, service, or product of some kind designed to solve the same basic problems. If not careful, it is easy to fall prey to the shiny toy syndrome.

In this context, the shiny toy syndrome occurs when we continuously alter our strategy and jump from one course of action to another because of a new attractive offering or solution. We are the most susceptible to falling for a shiny toy when we have stretch targets, and the work ahead seems daunting. The majority of the time, this unwelcome distraction results in higher effort and lower returns, and jeopardizes any previous progress. The shiny toy syndrome is a problem that needs to be avoided across any area of business or life.

More often than not, achieving results takes time. It requires us to build the right foundations, as discussed in the first few chapters of this book. If we do not have the right foundations, the shiny toy becomes all the more tempting. So especially with the amount of noise and distractions today, it's very important to stay the course.

A pivot, however, should not necessarily be confused with running after a shiny toy. A pivot is made when we alter the entire strategic direction due to a new variable or finding, and then execute consistently in that new direction—a concept discussed in the next section. The shiny toy syndrome instead alters the execution and strategy of your current direction in hopes of finding a silver bullet with the least amount of effort. It jumps back and forth between ideas and solutions to find a shortcut, and the cycle never stops.

Side Note:

As a football player, my weight would fluctuate between 275 and 295 pounds, depending on the year. Upon graduation, I decided to cut down my weight drastically. My first attempt didn't go so well. The first few weeks were great. I was following a training and nutrition plan, and I saw the numbers going down on the weight scale. Then I stumbled across a new fat-loss program for athletes. I dropped my existing workout plan and started following this new program. It worked for a week, but then I hit a plateau. Then I heard about a new diet that was guaranteed to help cut fat even quicker. I gave that a shot for a week or so, but it didn't do much for me. By this time, I was about a month and a half into my plan and didn't see any results. The cycle continued.

A few months later, I got accepted into the MBA program, and I had exactly six months before the semester started. The six months became somewhat of a milestone that allowed me to work backward from the September date. So I made a plan that included a fitness program, a diet plan with a caloric deficit, and intermittent fasting. I followed it consistently. At the end of every week, I would analyze whether I lost two to three pounds or if I needed to do something differently. Sometimes, I would alter the calorie deficit, change the intensity of my workouts, or at times just rest a little more. But I never changed the overall plan and strategy. Each month, I averaged twelve pounds of weight loss, and I hit my goal of being 215 pounds by September. The only difference was that this time around, I steered away from the shiny toy syndrome.

Sports to Business:

In sports, consistent execution comes down to the following:

1. **Team Execution**
   Teams executing and putting in the work every single day, aligned to their roadmaps and strategies. There are processes and rituals that the team follows day in and day out, with no compromise. Practices, meetings, game film reviews, and workouts are executed consistently according to the playbook.

2. **Individual Execution**
   Each athlete, coach, and member of the team personnel does their part on the field in practice, in training, and in meetings. They execute with determination and focus. Everyone also holds themselves accountable to put in the work at home or when they're alone.

   If we take an example of any two professional sports teams, the team that executes consistently will always beat a team that shows spurts of greatness, alongside slumps in performance.

   A team that can execute twenty plays back to back

with the same level of attention and detail will outscore a team that executes five phenomenal plays and fifteen sloppy ones. You can have the best talent, but even if one player misses his or her assignment, the other team will prevail. It takes disciplined, sound, fundamental execution until the clock hits zero.

Additionally, there are many games over the course of a season. It's common in pro sports where a mediocre team upsets the best team in the league in the regular season. The teams that go to the playoffs, however, are the ones that win the most games, not necessarily the ones that beat their longtime rivals but lose every other game during the regular season.

Championship teams play to their playbook, which helps them avoid the shiny toy. They prepare, practice, and win games based on their game plans. These teams stay true to their competitive advantages. Sometimes it's the type of offense or defense they run, sometimes it's the personnel, and sometimes it's their ability to adjust to the opponent at halftime.

Elite-level athletes prepare and execute week over week with consistency. It doesn't matter if the team is at the top of the standings. Great teams show up to practice, film sessions, meetings, and any other sessions with conviction and consistency. It adds up over time. Everyone on the team needs to show up and do the best they can every single day. You can't take a day off.

> Our defensive coordinator, Coach Knox, would always say that success equals preparation plus execution.
>
> And he was absolutely right. The weeks when we out-prepared our opponent, it didn't matter what tricks or plays they brought during the game, we were ready to shut them down. The level of detail Coach Knox expected during the week was second to none, and that allowed us to always be on our toes and be ready to capitalize on opportunities as they came.

In high-pressure, uncertain, and disruptive business settings, consistency will always win. Consistent execution comes down to the following:

1. **Team-Level Execution**
   Identifying the steps required to achieve high-level targets. These are objective and factual steps that one must undertake to achieve a desired result. This includes the daily connects, team stand-ups, communication protocols, work stream reviews, and strategy sessions. All must be executed to the plan.

2. **Individual Execution**
   Team performance is a product of individual performance. Every role and individual on the team contribute to the team's success. This is where everyone does their part by putting their team in the best position to win.

From personal preparation, processes, routines, and rituals to being disciplined and focused on whatever task it may be.

This also means doing the little things consistently that will give you a competitive advantage in the long run. Over the term of a year, doing something small for even ten minutes a day will add up. For example, reading a new book, researching your industry, or learning a new skill. If all you spend is ten minutes a day, but spend it consistently every single day, that becomes over sixty hours in a year. That's sixty hours of knowledge you now have that your colleagues or competitors don't.

Action Plan:

Winning the game of inches starts with great processes, rituals, and methodologies that can be repeated without much effort, willpower, or decision-making.

Here is a three-step plan to help you perform consistently and make big plays.

Step 1: Separate Actions from Results

Chapter 8 outlined the importance of breaking down the top-level goals into smaller chunks and aligning them to every team and individual in the company. In this step, go one level further and build out the key actions to achieving these priorities. It's great to have goals and perceived outcomes, but you need to separate them from the actions you need to take in order to achieve these goals and outcomes. Actions will keep your team marching forward and focused on the moment during tough stretches and chaos. They will keep you from obsessing over the results in the short term and from being tempted to bite at the shiny toy.

Take the 20 percent of the priorities from chapter 8 and break down key action items needed to achieve these priorities. The goal is to break down your large deliverables into smaller, digestible chunks. What are the key plays your team needs to make to get to your goal? For example, if your goal is to launch a new direct-to-consumer channel in the next six months, then your actions may include the following:

- Industry and competitive research
- Product analysis
- Building or launching an ecommerce platform with analytics
- Building a task force
- Running a pilot test

Continue to break these down further and assign owners and due dates to each. This will form your action plan.

Step 2: Build Systems and Anchors: Routines and Rituals

In sports, all you can control is the work you put in, not the scoreboard. Great athletes know that it's all about giving it their best each day, step by step. They know to focus on the processes that will in turn help them perform better when it's time to make big plays. And if they take care of execution, the results usually turn out in their favor.

Similarly, build systems and anchors that will allow you to execute on these actions consistently. Ask yourself these questions:

1. What do you personally need to do daily, weekly, and monthly to help you execute on your actions from step 1?
2. What do you need to do that is a repetitive team activity on a daily or weekly basis to keep you on track? Things such as weekly team calls to check status.
3. What do you need to do to become better at your job? Perhaps try reading an article every night or listening to a podcast once a week.

In a team setting, key rules and routines add consistency and accountability. For example, you can have a weekly team meeting where every owner presents their action items to the broader team. You can supplement it with regular check-ins at a one-to-one level with each of your team members to keep things moving forward, and to find out what kind of support they need on their journeys. Build tasks and processes that you and/or your team can execute consistently day in and day out. Remove the guesswork.

A team ritual that has proven to be very effective in my personal experience is a daily stand-up. In sports analogy, a stand-up is the extension of a huddle. It includes a daily fifteen-minute meeting with your team where everyone spends one to two minutes sharing what they did yesterday, what they are planning to do today, any roadblocks they foresee, and any help they might need. This is not a discussion forum or a troubleshooting meeting, rather an update to help align the team before execution begins. So as a leader, keep it on track and stay disciplined.

As a football team, every Sunday after the game we would show up to our meeting rooms and watch film on how we did. We would then take the learnings from the review sessions and apply them to our practices during the upcoming week. It didn't matter if we won by fifty points or lost the game, it was a process and a system that had to be followed. It is what allows teams to improve week over week.

Step 3: Evaluate Your Progress

As you execute your tasks and deliverables, find time to evaluate whether you're on the right path and adjust direction or tasks as needed. Make sure that the processes and systems are actually aligned with your goals. They should not be just making you feel productive on the surface but should be actually taking you closer to the destination.

At the individual level, you can start out by carving out some time once a week where you are reviewing your progress to ensure you're on track to delivering on the milestones within the time frame. Take a step back and evaluate whether the action items from step 1 are bringing you and your team closer to your goals. Measure your team's performance by evaluating whether the action items discussed last week were completed or if they're still open.

During our football season, each one of us, including the

coaches, would write down one thing we wanted to improve on during the week. We would write it on a big whiteboard near the locker-room entrance and read it before leaving for practice. It helped us see whether the work we were doing was helping us get better, but it was also a daily reminder to only focus on the things that would help us achieve the weekly goal. As our coaches would say in almost every practice, "Don't just go through the motions." This applies 100 percent in business as well.

Exercise:

- How would you rate your performance over the last twelve months? Have you been able to get consistent results? Or have there been highs and lows in your performance?

 ____

 ____

 ____

- What is the shiny toy syndrome, and what are some ways that you can avoid it from a personal or team standpoint?

 ____

 ____

 ____

- How do you personally trigger your team's performance on a day-to-day basis? Do you have regular one-to-ones? Do you regularly praise your team? Do you recognize success? Or is it something you only do as you see fit?

  ____

  ____

  ____

- Do you have a daily stand-up, or is communication something that only happens organically? What can you do to increase your level of communication?

  ____

  ____

  ____

As this chapter is heavy on consistent execution and systems, here is a quick cheat sheet on setting up and leading a project. I truly believe that we overcomplicate project management. It doesn't have to be that way. Here are the 20 percent of activities that you need to prioritize to effectively lead projects.

Step 1: Identify your goal—what is your major deliverable?
Step 2: Identify your scope—what is included in this deliverable and what is not?

Step 3: Identify major milestones you need to hit to complete this project.

Step 4: Build a list of tasks that will help you achieve each milestone.

Step 5: Assign a due date and an owner to each task.

Step 6: Connect with each owner to ensure you captured everything in steps 4 through 5.

Step 7: Present plan to key stakeholders to ensure alignment.

Step 8: Form a kickoff plan with all owners and stakeholders.

Step 9: Manage the project via a weekly update with task owners to ensure all is on track and to raise any risks.

Step 10: Provide an update to key stakeholders biweekly or monthly.

Keep it simple, work with people, and drive toward your goal.

CHAPTER 10

Celebrate Small Wins (and Failures)

The More You Celebrate, the More You Win!

In November 2018, I was watching the New York Giants face the Tampa Bay Buccaneers on TV. There is one play from that game that I sometimes revisit during long stretches at work. Early in the fourth quarter, the Giants were up 14–7, and the Bucs had the possession on their own eleven-yard line. Ryan Fitzpatrick, Bucs quarterback, threw a quick pass in hopes of moving the ball out of their own territory. But it was intercepted by Giants linebacker Alec Ogletree, and he ran it to the end zone for a defensive touchdown.

As Ogletree scored, he ran toward the fans in the end zone and started celebrating. He took a knee, and his fellow linebackers and defensive backs ran over, swarming around him, and joining him in the celebrations.

You could see about eight football players posing for celebratory pictures facing the Giants' end-zone crowd. As they were celebrating, in one corner of the screen you could also see the defensive linemen running toward the end zone. Within a few seconds, the entire defense was in the end zone posing for a celebratory team picture.

But it didn't stop there. As the entire defense was "getting their picture taken," players wearing dark-blue jerseys continued to pile on to this photo shoot. By this time you could also see offensive players join the party. These guys sprinted from the other side of the field, from the Giants' sideline all the way to the end zone to join their defense in the celebration. I counted about twenty players in the end zone before they ran back to the sidelines. You're only allowed to play with eleven players on the field at any time. Players who weren't a part of the play were joining the celebration.

They were celebrating as if they had won a big game. I couldn't believe it. The Giants' record coming into this game was 2-7. They had only won two games and were most likely going to miss the playoffs. But they played like a team that still believed in each other. They had one of the worst records in the NFL, but they played like champions. They did not give up hope. They wanted to be on the field. They cherished every moment of it. And they celebrated the small wins.

Great teams know that celebrating the journey is more important than celebrating the results.

I've also seen firsthand what celebrating can do for a losing team. In November of 2011, the college national championship game (the Vanier Cup) was paired up with the CFL final, the

Grey Cup game. Both were held at BC Place Stadium, two days apart. Our game was on Friday night, and the Grey Cup was on Sunday night. So I had the opportunity to watch two of the top football teams in Canada practice in preparation for the Grey Cup: the BC Lions and the Winnipeg Blue Bombers.

Both of the teams were meticulous, like an army that had been training for years, hitting every step in unison like a big, fast, well-oiled machine. But they were also calm, having fun, and enjoying the moment.

However, I remember seeing the Lions celebrate a lot more during practice. Perhaps it was because they were going to play for the Grey Cup at home in Vancouver, something not many players get to experience.

On Sunday night, when I watched the Grey Cup game, I saw that the same intensity, energy, and swagger that the Lions had in practice carried over to the game. They were making plays, having fun, but most importantly, celebrating every small play. The Lions made some big plays early and were up 14–6 at halftime. The Lions won that game 34–23.

In 2020, I spoke with one of the players who was on the Grey Cup winning team, James Yurichuk. I asked him what was different about the 2011 Lions team, from all other teams he played on. He said they actually started the 2011 season with five straight losses. They were the last in the league. But they knew deep down they were the best. They never stopped believing in each other and continued to have fun.

Instead of getting down on themselves, they focused on

getting better week over week, similar to the 2018 Giants defense. And they chose to celebrate the small wins. By the end of the season, they were a powerhouse.

The point is that many of us only celebrate and have fun when things go well. But we fail to celebrate the efforts, milestones, and outcomes on a daily basis. And we rarely celebrate our failures. The teams that win the big battles are the ones that celebrate the small wins. Sometimes it can be the deciding factor between winning and losing. The more you celebrate, the more you win.

Concept:

During long stretches when results are far and few, you need to celebrate the small wins. Celebration is enjoying the journey, breaking it up into digestible chunks, and rewarding yourself and your teams for the effort. It's simple and one of the most effective tools at boosting team performance and morale. It's about recognizing the positive strides on your journey. It also means celebrating the efforts, not just the results. This is a big one that most leaders overlook.

Being highly fixated on results undermines the effort that goes into achieving these objectives. Achieving stretch targets from chapter 1 is a result of consistent, iterative, and long-term focus and effort. Sometimes the effort yields results, and at other times, you need to adjust and pivot. If you wait a year to celebrate all the hard work, there is a high likelihood that you won't see things through. You'll stop enjoying what you're working on. Passion will turn into going through the motions. And the very thing that used to get you out of bed every morning will now start to feel like a burden.

Additionally, when we're executing and being pulled in multiple directions, it's tough to take a step back from the nitty gritty day to day. Most of the work we do in transformational times never yields results right away. It takes time. Many times we make progress, learn something valuable, and improve our approach, which are all positive steps forward on the journey. But it's hard to see the small wins when we're pushing hard with heads down. And we undermine these achievements because there is always more to do. Over time this leads to burnout and lower productivity.

At a team level, not celebrating the small efforts, milestones, and learnings significantly impacts morale, productivity, and overall performance. This leads to higher turnover and lower employee satisfaction. Therefore, celebration is crucial to sustaining performance and executing your plans.

Change is the new normal, and failure and iteration are a part of the process. So it's equally important to also celebrate failures. True innovation and leaps of success are usually preceded by numerous failures and iterations. Companies that have been thriving regardless of the circumstances or external environments all have a culture where people are encouraged to take risks. Risk-taking is encouraged through celebrating honest failures. Successful leaders and organizations celebrate what they can control, which is their effort and the process, and not the results. If the effort is there, then celebrate. Celebrate the learnings and readjust your approach. The results will come.

Celebrating small wins and failures along the journey will allow your team to push through obstacles and long stretches. It will help release the tension that builds up during high-pressure phases. It will help bring your team together. It will help you build a culture that will sustain you through peaks and valleys.

Celebrating feels good. And you do your best work when you feel good. So celebrate the small wins.

Side Note:

Celebration doesn't cost much. A monthly birthday celebration where you get a few cakes and some drinks for everyone goes a long way. So don't let budget hold you back from a culture of celebration. One time, I was leading a small team and we had zero budget. Literally no budget for anything that wasn't already preapproved. So I decided to pay out of pocket. It was a no-brainer. The team had been working hard, and the return that I got on that $150 in the long run was absolutely worth it.

Sports to Business:

Sports teams are notorious for celebrating. Every year there are numerous lists that count down the top fifty celebrations across all sports. It's just part of the game.

Here are two key takeaways from the world of sports:

1. **Celebrate the smallest of things**
   Take any sport—football, hockey, soccer, curling, you name it. You will see the players celebrate throughout

the entire game. They'll celebrate before the game starts and during the game when they score, make a good tackle, or make a save, because celebrating picks up the energy. It gets the team pumped up. It builds momentum. Sometimes you'll see a linebacker make a huge play, and that becomes the turning point in a game because the rest of the team feeds off the energy.

2. **Celebrate when no one is watching**
   Sports teams and athletes also celebrate behind the scenes. For example, after a game, everyone will go grab dinner together. We as the defensive line used to go and get a huge breakfast after every Sunday morning workout. It doesn't have to be something big, but it's important. Teams also celebrate in every single practice. They make it fun. Why? Because it is very difficult for a team to go through twelve to sixteen weeks of hard work, pushing toward the championship, and not have fun along the way. Injuries, stress, and ups and downs in a highly competitive, high-pressure atmosphere take a toll on the individuals and the team.

In a business setting, this means doing the following:

1. **Celebrate the journey**
   When leading a long-term initiative for a year or longer with no results till the end, a leader must break it up into milestones

and celebrate the small achievements throughout the timeline. This keeps the morale high and the journey enjoyable.

2. **Celebrate for fun**
   Sometimes, teams just need to have some fun by celebrating something that has nothing to do with the projects or results but is spontaneous. It gets everyone to relax a little and reset that tension, and brings you closer as a team. For example, Friday night drinks or a team event once a quarter.

3. **Lastly, celebrate your failures**
   This doesn't mean throwing a party after losing to a competitor. But if a team and everyone on that team gave it their best, then celebrate. If something didn't work out, but there were a few learnings along the way that helped fine-tune the strategy or execution, that to me is a win. Championship teams celebrate these moments. For example, an A/B test that did not outperform your control group but delivered some interesting insights about what type of messaging resonates best with your target market. Despite the results, you uncovered learnings that will make your future campaigns more effective.

Action Plan:

A senior executive at work once said to me, "Tanvir, the hardest thing won't be implementing the technology or dealing with issues when things go wrong. The hardest thing will be keeping your team's morale up during a year where you have a lot of work ahead of you with long days, with many setbacks, and where you will see no immediate results. So make sure you celebrate the journey." And that's exactly what we did.

Here is a four-step plan to start celebrating more to boost morale, increase productivity, and maximize overall performance.

Step 1: Break It Down

First, it's important to break down your projects, tasks, processes, responsibilities, and work streams into smaller chunks. Make a list of all the things your team is working on, then break it down into smaller chunks or deliverables. A good place to start are the actions from chapter 9. These should be key points in time that you will feel good about once you reach it. Look at your projects, overarching initiatives, product launches, anything that you and/or the team is working on that is a big priority.

Then break them down into deliverables that you believe are significant enough to celebrate. Do not confuse these for results. For example, if you're traveling from Toronto to New York by car, then these deliverables can be things such as packing your bags for the trip, filling up gas, getting snacks for the way, crossing the Canadian border, stopping for a quick break in Buffalo, and so forth. Think of them as simple actions that must be taken across the journey.

If your team is organized and has a good process in place for managing multiple projects, then you should already have these listed out in your plan. Once you identify these points in time, start planning how you can celebrate success or learnings for each of these. There's a big saying in sports: "One game at a time, one quarter at a time, one play at a time." It means focus on the task at hand and celebrate that moment.

The actions above also apply if you're leading an individual project. Whether it's delivering a massive report, building your dream car, or working on cutting down fifteen to twenty pounds, you must celebrate the small wins!

Step 2: Find Your Ambassadors

It's important to find the energy of your team. Usually there will be one or two people who will bring it day in and day out, every single day. Others will feed off of their energy. Give these ambassadors the autonomy and a budget to celebrate weekly or monthly.

This is something that is tough to do in a remote culture, when we're all on Zoom calls and dispersed across the globe. But don't let that excuse keep you from celebrating. Let the ambassadors get creative and try new things. I've found an element of surprise to work particularly well for remote settings. At the end of the day, have one person organize an "emergency" Zoom meeting and invite an unsuspecting teammate to join the call on the pretense of sorting out a last-minute mess. Once that teammate jumps on, they will be quite relieved to learn of the surprise! Now, the new teammate pays it forward and invites another colleague, and soon after you'll have the majority of the team on this call. This is a twist on a virtual happy hour, where you stop what you were doing, take a step back, and just enjoy the company of other humans and talk about something other than work.

Great coaches know that when they need the team to pick it up a notch, it starts with the captains. There are usually a handful of players that bring the hype. Whether it is with a touchdown celebration or a big interception, these players are the energy of the team. A single celebration can become the turning point in a game. Similarly, find your designated celebration captains.

Step 3: Jump Right In

It starts with you—lead the celebration. If your team failed, call it out and celebrate anyways—find something innovative. Unless you do it, others won't be inclined, especially if you have a culture that doesn't celebrate all that much today.

You need to be deliberate about celebrating and having fun because the impact you have as a leader on your team is immeasurable. The slightest of actions can impact a team's output for the day positively or negatively. So some days just kick it back and celebrate.

Be aware of when the team may need a pick-me-up or might be about to hit a wall. A leader must recognize this. Sometimes the best leaders simply turn it off for the day and give their teams a much-needed break.

If you've ever seen those viral videos of coaches dancing in the middle of a huddle, then you know what jumping right in means. If you haven't, then just search "football coaches dancing" on Google, and you'll see what I mean. Seeing a coach celebrate and dance is a lot more common than we think or see through the media. Great coaches know when the team needs a pick-me-up.

They know when the team needs a much-needed break after a long, hot practice during training camp.

Step 4: Deliberately Celebrate Failure

The chapter is incomplete without this point. If you miss this crucial step, then you'll fall short of building a great culture. A team needs to believe that celebrating efforts and milestones, regardless of the results, is something that is truly practiced, not just preached.

If you only celebrate the good times, teams will take fewer risks, and innovation will suffer. You'll run the risk of playing it safe and only doing things that are bound to be successful, which are usually things that worked in the past. In today's world, if you're not innovating and taking risks, then disruption is imminent.

This doesn't mean you promote failure. But once you have put guardrails and boundaries in place to a level that you're comfortable with, then it's all about the execution and being OK with mistakes along the way.

Find one thing every month that didn't work but was something that moved your team and organization forward. Maybe you ended up with a stronger team, saved costs along the way, learned something new about your customers, gathered invaluable data in the process, etc. If you learned something through the failure and can adjust and come back stronger, then celebrate!

When reviewing game film after a loss, we would still celebrate the things we did right as long as the effort was there. Usually as teams, whether in business or sports, we do most of the things well, and people generally put in the work. Wins and losses are sometimes decided over a very thin margin. Which means that it makes no sense to not celebrate the ninety-nine things that went right because of the one thing that went wrong.

For example, let's say you selected the number of calls booked as your sales team's KPI (key performance indicator) with the ultimate goal of increasing revenue. If you ended up shy of the revenue target but exceeded the target for the number of calls booked, then you should celebrate. Celebrate the failure, because your team maximized what they could control.

Celebrating small wins and failures will help you build the momentum needed to sustain performance. But celebration starts with you, and it starts with your mindset. So shift your mindset and celebrate!

Exercise:

Identify where you and your organization rank on celebration.

- List how many times either you or your team held a formal celebration in the last six months. I don't mean walking over to someone's desk and saying "great job," but actually making a plan to spend some time together to celebrate. How can you increase the frequency of celebrations?

  ____

  ____

  ____

- How often in the past twelve months was failure celebrated deliberately? Looking back, what failures do you believe should have been celebrated given the learnings and positive feedback they provided?

  ____

  ____

  ____

- Who on your team takes the initiative to celebrate? If that person leaves, will your culture change?

  ____

  ____

  ____

In this section, we covered how to maximize your execution and performance amid uncertainty and chaos by focusing on the right things and executing consistently, with the right mindset. The next section will focus on how to optimize your level of execution and make big plays during crucial moments.

SECTION 3

Postseason: Optimize and Win

P—Postseason
R—Regular season
O—Off-season

CHAPTER 11

Have a Short Memory

All You Can Control Is the Next Play

Forty-four years later, we were finally back, competing for the national championship title for just the second time in McMaster football history. It was November 25, 2011, and we were playing in front of over twenty-five thousand fans in Vancouver at The BC Place Stadium.

We had finally done it. All the hard work and dedication over the past four years had finally paid off. We beat the undefeated Western Mustangs to win our conference and then won the national semifinal against Acadia University. People didn't expect us to get this far. But here we were, competing for the Vanier Cup.

We continued to build on the momentum with a strong start to the game. We were up 23–0 at halftime. But the Laval Rouge et Or found their way back into the game. At the end of the fourth quarter, we were tied 31–31.

In the final minute of the game, we had a shot at winning with a thirty-yard field goal attempt. We were about to do something that had never been done before—win the Vanier Cup and be crowned national champions. We were about to make history.

I remember standing on the sidelines, watching the field goal team run out to the thirty-yard line. Tyler Crapigna was our all-star kicker who had been clutch for us the entire season. He got ready to kick the game winner.

Tyler was kicking from the thirty-yard line, a distance from which he rarely missed. He had kicked in high-pressure situations before throughout the season. I never totally understood what went through a kicker's mind when the game was riding on their shoulders, but Tyler always made it look easy.

Tyler was all set in his stance, ready for the center to snap the ball. He put his hand up, signaling everyone on the field to get ready for the snap. The stadium went quiet. The center snapped the ball. The snap looked good. Tyler kicked the ball. He missed.

And now we were headed into overtime, against the number one ranked team in the country.

For a kicker, that is very disheartening. The opportunity to win a game in front of one of the largest crowds in Canadian university football, to do what had never been done before in history, but not being able to capitalize on it is heartbreaking. He had the perfect chance to beat the best team in the league in theatrical fashion to sum up our season—but he missed the uprights.

None of us could imagine what it must've felt like for him to miss that kick. Only he knows. He missed a field goal that he had made thousands of times during practice. It's really tough to shake it off.

With the missed field goal, the fourth quarter ended, and we were headed into overtime tied at 31–31. In overtime each team would receive one set of downs. Whoever scored the most points per possession would win. If the game was still tied at the end of each round, then both teams would receive another fresh set of downs until someone outscored.

During the first round of possessions, both teams scored a touchdown. The game was tied yet again, at 38–38.

In the second round, Laval had the first possession, and we intercepted the ball. Now it was up to our offense to win the game. And just like at the end of the fourth quarter, Tyler Crapigna once again found himself standing on the field. He had another shot at a game-winning field goal.

In this moment, Tyler could have dwelled on the past, engaged in negative self talk, and crumbled under pressure. Or he could have shaken it off and capitalized on the opportunity that lay ahead.

Tyler put his hand up again, ready to kick the field goal. Once again the crowd went quiet. The snap was good. Tyler kicked the ball. And this time, he made it.

With that kick we made history, winning the first-ever national championship as the McMaster Marauders.

Concept:

Once you're in crunch time, you need to keep marching forward despite failures or setbacks. Having a short memory means not allowing a past, unfavorable event or failure to affect your future performance. It requires us to analyze the past event by detaching ourselves from the results and failures and by identifying key learnings to carry with us into the future.

When you fail in business, it can be tough to shake it off. You may get caught up on past failures. Your performance may suffer. There may be a lingering doubt about a recent failure that stays in the back of your head. But the only value that can be extracted from dwelling on past failures is pinpointing what went wrong, and how such misses can be avoided in the future. Past failures do not dictate future performance. You might miss a shot, but you'll have a crack at it again. And you need to be ready to capitalize on that opportunity.

Rebounding with a short memory is about not dwelling on a recent failure or miss by consciously removing any negative emotions or memories from that event. It's about minimizing stress, maintaining confidence, and continuing to execute at peak performance. It's about taking the feedback needed from the past event and adjusting your performance in the future in an objective manner.

This applies at a team level and at an individual level. As a team, it means not letting a recent loss derail you from your next game or upcoming project. It's about not letting a loss hurt your team morale, lower your team confidence, or impact your overall performance in a negative way. At an individual level, it means learning from something in the past that didn't go well, such as a presentation, a bad project, or maybe even a bad year, and adjusting your performance for the future. The key is to analyze, learn, and move on with the same or even higher levels of confidence than before.

In a business environment where uncertainty is high, competition is intense, and the speed of execution needs to be fast, mistakes and failures are common. In fact, great organizations and leaders encourage failures and risk-taking as these principles lead to breakthrough performance. If we're afraid to make mistakes, then we will shy away from unconventional, risky approaches and will be content with playing it safe. Which means in a world where we need to reinvent ourselves to beat disruption, we will be mediocre at best, and at the mercy of other innovators. Thus, short memory is crucial to success in disruption.

There are two types of failures.

I believe there are two types of failures, which I call missed-play failures and missed-season failures. A missed-season failure is when you miss a long-term goal or objective, whereas a missed-play failure is falling short on one or more of the smaller initiatives designed to take you closer to achieving that long-term goal or objective.

The key is to understand that missed plays do not necessarily result in losing the season or failing to achieve your long-term goals. In fact, in my experience, missed-play failures have actually helped me reach my macro goals. I view missed-play failures as a part of execution.

For example, a macro goal of increasing revenue by 50 percent over the previous year may include numerous plays or micro objectives such as new marketing campaigns or product launches in an effort to meet the overarching revenue target. In this scenario, a missed-season failure would be falling short of the 50 percent revenue increase, whereas a missed-play failure would be falling short on some of the marketing campaigns or product initiatives designed to meet the 50 percent incremental revenue target.

Missed-play failures simply act as feedback for your overall strategy. They validate whether or not you're on the right track and if any adjustments or iterations need to be made along the way. Numerous external and unprecedented factors emerge in business over the course of a strategic plan. Fast execution and feedback help you stay ahead of the curve by testing different products or solutions, learning about the market and your competitors, validating your assumptions and hypotheses, and allowing you to adjust much faster than others.

Consider the example of an online shoe store. Launching a beta-version shoe-comparison feature on the store app with the goal of increasing online conversions may or may not result in direct sales. It will, however, provide ample data on how customers are behaving and, if analyzed correctly, their underlying needs. In fact, data may show that sales of a particular shoe skyrocketed, while sales of another shoe declined, which may be a complete surprise for your team. Having customer feedback from this minor test, even if it doesn't result in higher sales (missed-play), will allow your team to unpack customers' underlying behaviors and learn about what they really want. This will, in turn, allow you to reevaluate and iterate, for example, your brand positioning, marketing spend, and growth strategy.

The key here is that as leaders and as individuals, we must separate the missed-play failures from the missed-season failures and treat the former as just a part of execution. While doing so, we need to ensure that our teams and people practice a short memory and continue to learn and move forward.

Sports to Business:

In sports, there are constant failures, day in and day out. That is why teams practice—to learn from their mistakes and get better every single day. They practice short memory.

We can break down having a short memory into two buckets:

1. **At the Individual Level**
   Every player makes mistakes. You might not see it from the sidelines, but no one ever has a perfect game. There are numerous plays in a single game, and it's near impossible for any one player to have a perfect game. In a basketball game, for example, players miss shots, sometimes miss an open layup, and at times turn over the ball with just a few seconds left on the clock. But seldom ever will you see a great player hang his or her head after missing

an open shot. If it doesn't go in, he or she sprints back to play defense without letting the previous missed-play failure affect their future performance.

2. **At the Team Level**

   From a team standpoint, the missed-play failures are a part of the game. These smaller failures don't necessarily mean you've lost the game. Maybe someone is having a bad day shooting from the three-point line. Great coaches recognize this and make adjustments on the team to help give this player a better chance, boost confidence, or perhaps even give him or her a break.

   Moreover, losing a game or two during a long season does not mean you're not a championship-caliber team. Great teams learn from losses and bounce back stronger. It's all about learning, adjusting, and moving forward.

In business, it all comes down to how you react to a failure or mistake. You can either learn from it and continue marching forward with a positive attitude, or let that mistake affect your future performance.

Having a short memory in business falls into the following two buckets:

1. **At the Individual Level**

   Missed plays are inevitable. As an individual, you need to analyze the results, take what's important, and move forward with confidence. Things fall through the cracks, a presentation gets ripped apart at the board meeting, or you lose a big client—it happens. Bouncing back requires learning and focusing on the opportunities ahead.

2. **At the Team or Organization Level**
   Successful leaders encourage and enable the team to shake off the small failures and continue marching forward. A botched project or unsuccessful product should not deter a team or an organization from trying again. Recognize what didn't work at the team level, iterate, and get back after it. The reality of disruption and intense competition is that you might lose some big games. And that's OK. Learn, shake it off, and boost your team to come back stronger.

   Regardless of the role you play—an individual contributor, a leader, or a teammate—you need to forgive yourself for past mistakes. Otherwise, you risk not just hurting your own performance but jeopardizing the performance of your entire team.

Side Note:

I was leading a global project, and my job included managing a cross-functional team of over twenty members, dispersed across two continents. From the get-go, it was a high-risk project without enough time, resources, or budget.

It was early in my career, and I didn't think much of the risks in the beginning. I thought that because no one else seemed to be raising any red flags, we would be fine. So I started executing with what I had. We tried our best but came up short. The leadership team was not happy. It was a complete mess. It did take a toll on me, and I considered quitting. I started to get down on myself, while blaming others and finding excuses. I didn't believe it was my fault. I felt like it was a project that was never going to succeed from the get-go.

A few weeks later, after things settled down, I decided this was not going to be my last project. The failure wasn't a reflection on my abilities. I wasn't going to let one mistake ruin my growth, my future performance, or my track record. Instead of dwelling on the mistakes I had made and deflecting blame, I decided to separate myself from the results. I objectively analyzed what I could have done better in that situation. I took away four critical lessons:

- I could have raised my hand up front and discussed the risks.
- I could have pushed harder on getting additional resources.
- I could have forced all stakeholders to align up front with a clear scope, deliverables, and expectations across departments.

- And I could have kept a positive attitude, which would've helped fix the issues a lot sooner.

When a similar project came up again just three months later (fortunately, the leadership team still believed in me), it was my shot at redeeming myself. I applied those four learnings up front to a project that also seemed impossible from the get-go. But this project became one of my most successful deliverables of the year, directly adding eight figures in revenue to the company's bottom line.

Action Plan:

Here's a five-step process to practice building a short memory.

Step 1: Start at the Organization Level

Before we can encourage and build a short memory system for our teams, we need to first make it clear that failures and mistakes are part of the game. This is a foundational element that must be addressed. Fear of judgment from colleagues and leadership will result in a culture of "playing it safe." Having a recent project or initiative perceived as a failure can seriously damage a team member's confidence, morale, and motivation. It holds people back from pursuing true innovation. In fact, it encourages a culture of complacency, which is a recipe for disaster.

Therefore, leaders need to instill confidence in their teams, making it clear that failing along the way is acceptable. It's not enough to simply communicate this—leaders must embody the culture and lead by example. One way of doing this is by publicly recognizing key initiatives that did not go as planned and sharing the results and learnings of the effort with the broader team. Speaking about key learnings and the long-term impact a project had on the season win or macro goal, despite any mediocre short-term results, will illustrate the importance of fast execution and create an environment where people feel safe.

You should also consider reflecting on missed-play failures annually. It will put into perspective the impact fast execution had on the overall objective, which is sometimes tough to see without the bird's-eye view of the larger initiative. A great sports coach will never yell at his or her team for losing if the team played their hearts out. Focus on the effort versus results and build this into your culture.

Step 2: Separate Execution from Reflection

You can't let emotions and negativity come along with you for the ride. When you make a mistake during a game, during a project that is moving really fast, during a presentation to the board of directors, or when firefighting a crisis, you need to always look forward. It is of no use to start thinking about what went wrong when you're still in execution mode. If you start thinking about a mistake while you still need to perform with 100 percent focus, it will affect your performance and sabotage the remaining task.

Therefore, as leaders and individuals, we need to train our teams, and train ourselves, to separate execution mode from learning mode. We must leverage our game faces and focus on the task at hand. The more we can train ourselves on this, the easier it will get to not dwell on mistakes while you're executing. Once the execution is over, then we can focus on what went wrong, what to learn, and how to fix it.

Step 3: Detach Yourself from the Outcome

Do not let mistakes and failures affect or change your confidence levels or positive mindset. Most missed shots are not a reflection of ourselves but merely an error in execution or a result of uncontrollable, uncertain external variables.

Therefore, if you are dwelling on a mistake, it's important to take a step back and view yourself from a third person's point of view. This will help you leverage facts and data on what went wrong, and how the "person" who made this mistake can fix it moving forward. It helps remove any emotions or biases out of the equation.

What I personally find helpful is to give myself the role of a consultant hired by "Tanvir" to analyze his performance and objectively state key next steps. It helps me keep the emotions aside and objectively focus on the outcome with a holistic approach, as if I was helping someone else.

Step 4: Learn for the Future

As you analyze your past performance, identify the top three learnings that will put you in a better position to make the play in the future. The key is to only prioritize the learnings that will be the most beneficial to you in the future. Don't be fixated on the nice-to-haves that don't necessarily add value. Focus on the meat (or veggies for my vegan friends).

For example, if you are analyzing your presentation that didn't go well and you realize that your slides need improvement, you didn't effectively use body language, and that you didn't know an answer to a technical question that was out of scope, then focus on the first two as those will directly help you improve future presentations. You can spend time learning the third point, but it won't add any value for future presentations, given the topic that was out of scope and not critical to your business or deliverables.

Focus on the core skills that will allow you to maximize your performance in the future.

Step 5: Shake It Off

Once you've analyzed your past performance and learned the keys for future improvements, it is time to shake off any negative feelings or emotions that you had with the previous performance. You've learned what you could, and it's time to move on.

I compare it to a nice, relaxing cooldown stretch at the end of a long, hard workout. After you put your body through rigorous exercise, you take some time to lengthen your muscles and flush out the lactic acid. When you leave the gym, you feel lighter and regain your mobility. Shaking off a bad performance after you've taken what you can from the learnings should make you feel lighter and get you back on your horse.

Focus your energy on visualizing how you will use the

learnings to better perform in the future when you're presented with a similar situation.

This is where it's important to have a positive attitude. There is too much negativity all around us. If you're hanging around with people at work who are still dwelling on their past mistakes, then you need to tell them to stop or separate yourself from the conversation. Protect your thoughts and stay positive. Visualize future success.

Exercise:

Here are a few questions to help rebound from failure and keep a short memory:

- How can you better separate missed-play failures from missed-season failures?

  ____

  ____

  ____

- How can you increase your team's threshold of accepting and rebounding from mistakes during execution?

  ____

  ____

  ____

- Do you find yourself dwelling on a recent failure? Have you separated the facts from emotions? What did you learn from the failure?

  ____

  ____

  ____

CHAPTER 12

Pivot and Adjust

No Game Plan Survives Four Quarters

Our upcoming opponent in a regular-season game was a team with a very mobile quarterback. This quarterback ran more than he passed and was causing all sorts of problems for teams across the league. He could throw, he could run, and he was hard to predict. Most of the time, he would make a decision after the snap as to whether he would pass or run. A very dangerous threat.

Everything we had been taught as defensive linemen was actually counterproductive against this quarterback. During a passing play, the defensive linemen are taught to pin their ears back, explode out of their stance, and get to the quarterback as quickly as possible. It's called a pass rush (see figure 1). During our first practice in preparation for the game, our defensive line coaches did a demonstration to show us why this wasn't going to work.

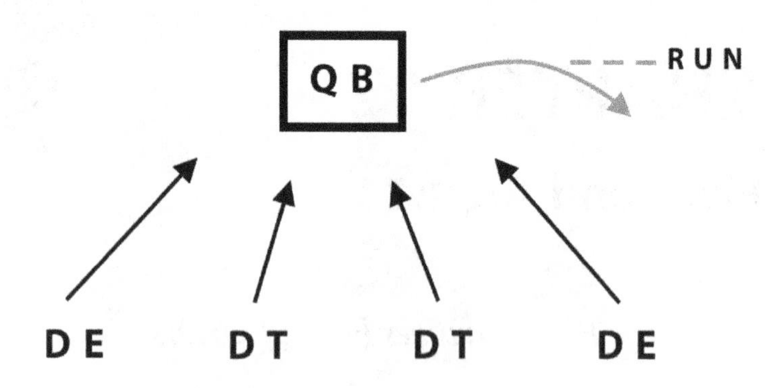

Figure 1: A regular pass rush

The coaches asked one of the receivers from the offense to pretend to be the quarterback. Then, they asked the four of us to do what we were taught to do: sprint as fast as possible toward the quarterback and pretend to tackle him. The coach said, "Hut," and we exploded off the line. Just as we started sprinting toward the quarterback, he faked a pass. He pretended to throw the ball (pump fake) but pulled it back. It made us all jump midway in our sprint to try to knock down the pass, which he never threw. It was a simple instinct on our end.

As he had us fooled, he took a few really hard steps to his right, signaling that he was going to run toward the sidelines. As we recovered from our jump, we started sprinting toward our left as fast as we could. We thought this time it was going to be a simple race to cut the quarterback off before he got to the sidelines. And just as we were running full speed toward the sidelines, he planted his right foot and changed direction again. All four of us missed and ran right by him, and he had the entire left side of the field open to run. If this was a real game, we would have given up an easy twenty-to-thirty-yard run, and potentially a touchdown.

That drill made it clear that whatever we had been doing was not going to work against this quarterback come Saturday. This was an anomaly, and we would need to adjust our game plan to match his style of play. So our coaches made a few adjustments to our game plan.

First, instead of running after the quarterback with blinders on, we pressed forward in a controlled manner. Our first priority was to contain him inside an imaginary box. We were less focused on getting to him for a sack, and in turn forced him to pass the ball. We had a strong squad of defensive backs and linebackers and felt confident that they would win the one-on-one battles against their receivers during passing plays. We called it the box-and-pinch technique (see figure 2).

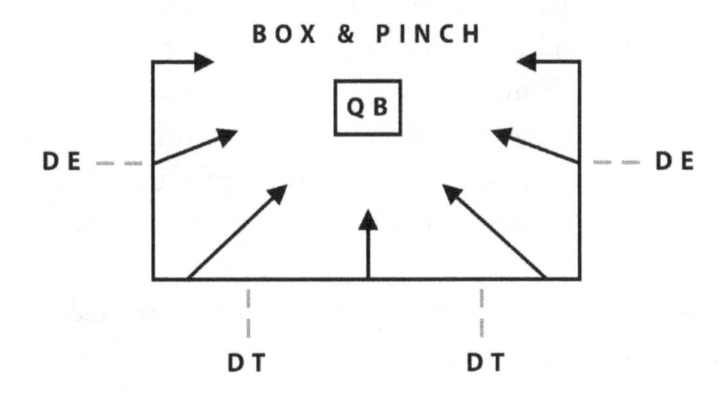

Figure 2: A pass rush with the box and pinch technique

Second, on most plays there would be a linebacker or a defensive lineman shadowing the quarterback in case he got out of our imaginary box and found a running lane. This individual would be responsible to track down the quarterback and minimize any damage.

On game day, that's how we started the game. We were disciplined. We stayed in our lanes. We boxed and pinched. This took away the quarterback's running options and forced him to throw the ball from the pocket. Our defensive backs won most of the passing battles. And we won the game.

We had one of the best defenses in our conference leading up to the game. But it would have been a big mistake if our coaches tried to shut this team down with our base playbook. We had to respect the competition. We had to adjust. In fact, this was not the only team where we had to change our entire defensive game plan. Especially in the postseason/ playoffs, great teams would watch enough film to pick up our tendencies. They would draw up new plays that we had never seen before on film. Which meant we had to learn how to make adjustments midgame. Because we had mastered the basic playbook and could execute it with consistency (sections 1 and 2), it enabled us to counterattack and adjust within a matter of minutes.

Great leaders and teams build the ability to pivot and adjust as part of their playbook.

Concept:

Nothing in life is predictable. You need to be prepared to adjust to factors outside your control in order to continue pushing toward your target. Pivoting and adjusting is about altering the direction, processes, and priorities of a business to respond to external factors or new learnings, while minimizing any negative effects on speed, core business, team morale, and operational effectiveness.

Pivots should be expected and need to be built into the strategic roadmap. Pivots and adjustments can range from adjusting your project plan to deciding to drop a product line to changing your sales pitch to altering your four-year strategic plans.

You may have been hearing the word pivot more and more over the past few years. Traditional long-standing businesses and teams have had to pivot their product roadmaps, leadership teams have had to pivot their strategic roadmaps, and as a whole, numerous businesses have had to pivot their operating and business models. As we've discussed, there will continue to be new entrants in the market, industry disruption is going to become even more common, competition is going to get fiercer, and consumer demands will continue to rise. Hence, pivots need to be a part of every business playbook.

At a granular level, teams need to pivot their direction or adjust their execution due to changing customer demands, competitive pressures, or internal changes. For example, if you're a car manufacturer and your competitor just unveiled four new financing options, whereas you have none, you'll have to adjust. Or if you saw an opportunity to capture customers who demand voice ordering through Alexa and Google, then your digital roadmap may change. Or if at the retail store level the frontline staff are having a difficult time operating the new pin pads, then you'll need to prioritize this issue over others.

At a macro level, over the past twenty-five to thirty years, many businesses that have been able to thrive in the face of unseen threats, disruption, and market volatility share a unique operating principle: they've never been afraid to change direction. For example, Netflix started off as a mail-in DVD service, but when streaming picked up given the internet boom, they were quick to scrap their existing business model and go all into streaming. Or the Walt Disney Company when they acquired Pixar and Marvel in the 2000s to reignite growth and profitability in a new sector. Or Amazon, which went from an online bookstore out of a garage to virtually selling everything including fresh food with same-day delivery. When we look closely, their technology is something that others can copy. What actually allows them to thrive is their ability to constantly adjust and deliver what the consumers demand.

The reason most tech companies like Netflix are able to adapt and have become the golden standard for speed and agility is not because they have people who are generally faster or more agile. It's because pivots and adjustments are simply part of their day to day. They are built with nimbleness at the core. Their playbooks include adjustments. And although it may seem like the tech companies are fast, what really sets them apart is their ability to launch, take risks, test, gather data, and iterate while being OK with a subpar product at first.

As leaders are tasked with transformations, doing more with less, and needing to adapt and move faster, the best ROI on one's time is to take a step back and build pivots and adjustments into their operating plans. Then it's a matter of building the system where the team can execute with agility.

Pivoting every so often can cause chaos.

Chaotic environments are known as culture killers and generally have high turnover. But while chaotic environments are usually fast paced, fast-paced environments with numerous pivots and turns need not be chaotic.

For example, maybe you've experienced chaos when the marketing team decided to change the launch date of a new product at the last minute, resulting in a lot of firefighting for your tech or operations teams. Or when you were about to pilot a new feature at your retail locations, and the operations team pushed back. Or when there was a pressing issue that had to be resolved at the customer level, and your support team was getting bombarded with tickets, but it wasn't a priority on the tech roadmap.

There are three main drivers of this type of chaos in a fast-paced environment:

1. Customer demands—operating in an industry where frictionless experiences are upping one another, and demands are rising

2. Competitive rivalry—new entrants disrupting your market, or operating in an industry with low margins or price wars, or in a volume-based business that is highly volatile
3. Internal processes—ways of doing things or departments that are still the same as they were ten years ago and are now being asked to adapt and change

If customer demands, competitive rivalry, or existing processes are putting pressure on the business to pivot and change, then it's important to address these three areas with proper planning, internal alignment, and expectations. You need to get ahead of it and make the necessary adjustments.

Sports to Business:

Sports are synonymous with competition. Competition pushes opponents to try new strategies and plays. A team can prepare as much as possible for the game. Teams can cook up the best strategies, creative plays, awesome counterattacks, and new game plans. But come game day, all it takes are a few unlucky bounces, and you're back on your heels in unknown territory.

Therefore, sports teams need to adjust all the time—during the season, during the game at halftime, midplay. The ability to adjust successfully starts with the following:

1. **Having the Right Fundamentals**

   Pivoting and adjusting on the fly require a strong understanding of the basic playbook. To adjust to complex schemes, the players first need to execute the core plays to near perfection and know their individual assignments. You can't run before you learn how to walk.

2. **Encouraging Risk-Taking**
   Adjusting requires trying out new things—oftentimes there is no guarantee whether the new play calls will work against an opponent. But great teams execute without fear of failing. If something doesn't work out, they adjust again.

3. **Making Quick Decisions**
   There is very little time during a game or in between plays to gather data and analyze whether the new adjustment is the best one. Great teams and coaches make quick decisions and execute. The players on the field never contemplate the play. They pick a direction and go full speed.

4. **Building Confidence and Trust**
   For a team to adjust, there needs to be confidence and trust in each other as teammates and coaching staff. It does a team no good if the players don't trust each other or don't believe in the coach's decision.

Business playbooks require constant adjustments to handle disruptive and competitive pressures. Organizations need to pivot and adjust at multiple levels, sometimes at the strategic level, sometimes at the team level, and sometimes at the execution level. The analogy from adjusting and pivoting starts with the following:

1. **Having the Right Fundamentals**
   Having the right foundations, alignment, and core skill sets within the organization (section 1). This includes a long-term strategy based on careful planning, as well as foundational work behind the scenes to enable pivots and adjustments down the road. This also includes the skill sets at an individual level and at the team level. If the marketing team shifts its strategy from a retail to direct-to-consumer channel, then having the right tech and ops skill sets and alignments is important.

2. **Encouraging Risk-Taking**
   Business is much more unpredictable than sports. It's tough to fully analyze the factors outside of one's control, which at times makes it hard to pull the trigger. Unlike sports, the rules of business keep changing. Therefore, pivoting requires a culture where risk-taking and making mistakes is seen as part of doing business. It is a major success factor in competing against nimbler, faster, and disruptive new entrants.

3. **Making Quick Decisions**
   The ability to make decisions and pick a new direction is a must. The companies that adjust faster and quicker, while not being perfect, find themselves in stronger

competitive positions. Great leaders make decisions when they feel 70 percent certain. It allows them to move faster, learn, iterate, and adjust ahead of the competition.

4. **Building Confidence and Trust**
   Pivoting at fast speeds requires aligning multiple work streams and projects. Having the confidence and trust in each other as teammates, leadership, and colleagues is necessary to pivot at high speeds. Businesses are large entities with multiple layers and inputs, which become hard to navigate if there is lack of trust between teammates.

Action Plan:

Before diving into the action plan, here is an activity to evaluate your level of readiness to pivot and adjust amid disruption and chaos:

1. Think of a scenario where your entire team has to pivot to something completely different. An example of this could very well be something we've all been through—the pandemic. It can also be in response to a sudden announcement from a tech giant who decides to enter your line of business, or it can be where your project budget gets cut in half, and you're still expected to deliver on time.
2. With your current team members, resource availability, and relationships, identify whether or not you can deliver on the following based on the new strategic direction:

- New customer demands
- New competitive pressures
- Executing within existing internal processes

3. If you feel confident about number two above, then identify if you can change direction and start executing in a new direction within a week, with no turnover or pushback and a minimal hit to morale. If not, then it's time to work on your own "goal-line drill."

The goal-line drill is a football drill where a defense plans for high-risk scenarios. Before each game, coaches put together contingency plans based on what the other team might show when the defense is in an unfavorable position. An example scenario is when, if the other team's offense is on our one-yard line in the fourth quarter, a yard away from the end zone, and if they score, they win the game.

This is a high-pressure, high-stress situation that a defense does not want to be in. But the point of the drill is to be ready for the worst-case scenarios, especially when it may come down to winning or losing the game.

So how does a football team prepare for their goal-line drill?

1. The defensive coaches identify vulnerable situations that the team may find itself in. For example, winning by four points with two minutes remaining, and the other team

has the ball, is on our one-yard line, and could win the game if they score.

2. The defensive coaches shortlist three to four possible plays that the opposing team may run when in the situation above. The coach looks at what the team has run before in previous games, and what might they want to exploit based on our system of play. This also includes studying the plays in detail, including things such as any personnel changes they make in these situations, their past success, and tendencies based on data from previous games.
3. The defensive coaches build counterplays for the defense to attack the offense in these unfavorable positions. In the example above, to stop the offense from scoring.
4. Positional coaches and players then practice these counterplays to prepare and be ready for if this ever happens in a game. Sometimes, different players are substituted during these plays and include different techniques based on what the offense runs. It becomes a matter of preparing through both physical and mental repetitions so that it's nothing new come game time.
5. When it's game time, and a defense finds themselves in this situation, everyone knows exactly how to counterattack, who needs to be on the field, and what the individual assignments are. From there, it's just a matter of execution.

The beauty of a goal-line drill is that even though it seems like a last-minute adjustment, the thought process, resources, direction, and execution were already part of the plan.

How can you build your own goal-line drill in business? Here is a five-step plan.

Prep Step: Revisit Your Playbook

Your playbook from chapter 2 is a prerequisite to pivoting and adjusting during the postseason. Building a playbook that takes into account your long-term vision alongside investments into building key foundations will allow you to pivot and adjust when needed. If you feel your playbook does take into consideration the future macro environment and competitive forces, and/or is not built with strong foundations from section 1—then revisit chapter 2. Otherwise, pivoting and adjusting will result in chaos, noise, lack of alignment, lower productivity, lower team morale, and turnover, among other things.

Step 1: Identify Possible Scenarios

You need to identify the worst-case scenarios that you may face as a leader, a CEO, a project leader, or as an individual contributor. Based on your current direction and strategy, start brainstorming what types of situations you may find yourself in that you don't want to be in.

Look at industry trends, where your customers are headed, competitive pressures, similar businesses, and anything else that may help. A good place to start is by splitting this into two categories: external and internal.

For external, look at what outside threats may put you in a negative position, such as losing a big client, a PR blunder, a new entrant, etc. For internal, look at what in your current organization can put you in an unfavorable position, such as losing someone highly talented, a safety incident, a cyberattack, etc.

Summarize the top three scenarios that you believe you may face and need to prepare for.

____

____

____

Step 2: Strategic Alignment

Identify what changes will need to be made at the strategic level for the business if one of the above scenarios was to come true.

If the scenarios are highly likely to occur, are there new objectives that need to be introduced today to the strategic plan to make these a priority?

For example, if you believe your business will need to counter highly capable startups entering and disrupting the industry in a matter of time, then getting all senior leaders aligned cross-functionally will give you time to prepare and make necessary adjustments in each business unit or department.

I've also seen a huge benefit in getting marketing, technology, and operations aligned up front. If you're adjusting anything that is customer facing and includes an online, tech, or e-commerce component, then these three departments must work as one unit. Having one move faster than the other will only cause chaos and slow things down further.

Some pivots and adjustments require work up front, and a big reason why organizations have a hard time pivoting and adjusting is due to lack of communication and alignment. Therefore, identify the key stakeholders that will be impacted by your pivots based on your scenario planning and get them on board. Shift your processes, break down silos, and open up communication.

When a team practices the goal-line drill, everyone on the field and on the sidelines needs to understand the counterattack. The smallest of change impacts your teammates even if they are not directly involved in the new plan. So communication is key.

Step 3: Team Alignment

Now identify key players in your existing team who will need to shift their focus, take on a new initiative, or take on a completely new role as a result of the shift. Then communicate the strategy, possible changes, and any training required to best prepare. This applies to anyone, whether you're a department head, a cross-functional leader, or an analyst who manages an external vendor team.

The only way you'll be successful in maintaining speed and pivoting in a disruptive environment is if your entire team is ready, capable, and understands the direction and expectation. Keep transparency at the forefront. As long as everyone knows what is required and expected of them in a certain situation, execution will become easy. Align with clear expectations and eliminate any guesswork.

Step 4: Resource Availability

During a goal-line play in an actual game, you'll see different players coming on the field versus those who were in the previous plays. This is because the players needed to stop an offense from scoring at the goal line are different from the ones who were needed to cover a fifty-yard pass. The ones at the goal line are a lot bigger to match the size and strength of the big offensive linemen, whose only job is to push the defense into their own end zone, making way for a touchdown.

Similarly, based on your possible counterattacks, identify any additional or different people you'll need, as well as any other capital investments or partnerships to successfully execute and lead in times of uncertainty. Then go and seek out the resources you need to shift direction and adjust. You may need to seek leadership buy-in or work on aligning yourself on projects where you can tap into shared resources. In either case, start early and plan ahead.

Step 5: Pull the Trigger and Mobilize

The final step to pivoting with and adjusting it to pull the trigger (a.k.a. make the decision). Once you're ready with your plan of attack, you need to commit and execute at full speed.

In one of our workshops that we run for corporate teams, we go over a concept known as "Decision-Making in a Digital World." We cover three steps to making effective decisions as leaders and teams that allow companies to move faster and get better results. (You can learn more about our workshops at www.tanvirbhangoo.com.)

First is processing the information, second is problem-solving, and the last step is pulling the trigger. Diving into the last step, if you cannot pull the trigger, all the planning and preparation goes to waste.

How can you pull the trigger and commit?

First, the team or individual that is making the decision needs to be empowered. They need to have the autonomy and belief from the leadership team to do their best work. Second, they need to be confident. Confident in themselves but also confident in their team to know they have each other's backs in case things don't work out. Lastly, the decision needs to be made at full speed. Think of a linebacker before the ball is snapped, a tennis player waiting to return the serve, or a hockey goalie facing a two-on-one scenario. These athletes cannot hesitate, second-guess their decision or the direction they chose to pursue, or have doubts in their teammates' abilities to do their individual jobs. They need to commit.

Sometimes, pivoting and changing direction means deciding to commit to things before we're fully ready. The reality is that when things are moving fast, you'll seldom ever feel fully ready to pull the trigger. But it's more costly to not make a decision than it is to make a wrong decision. Great athletes and leaders make a decision, commit, and adjust. Most of the time it's better to take a shot, miss, and shoot your own rebound than it is to not take a shot at all.

Oftentimes, we only need 20 percent of the data we think we need, and our strategies and decisions rarely ever use 100 percent of the data that we have collected. For example, trying to collect data on what your consumers may want to buy as an upsell item before launching your online ordering website to begin with is practically worthless. It makes sense to first launch your digital sales channels and tackle the upsell later. Why? Because, one, the upsell has no dependency on you launching your new website. You can simply launch the new website first and start generating revenues. And two, through these online transactions, you'll actually have real, better-quality data that you can then use for adding the upsell feature in the next update.

Exercise:

- What is a goal-line drill in business, and how can you build one for your team and organization? What are some steps that you can take today to build your contingency plan?

  ____

  ____

  ____

- What allows tech-first companies to operate faster and nimbler than traditional companies? How can you apply these principles to your business or team?

  ____

  ____

  ____

- Do you or your team find it difficult to pull the trigger and make decisions during moments of high pressure? What are some steps that you can take to fully commit despite the lack of information or data?

  ____

  ____

  ____

CHAPTER 13
Build Your Depth Chart

It's Not a Rebuild, It's a Reload

During our 2012 season training camp, the *Hamilton Spectator* published an article titled "Marauder Defensive Line Takes a Hit." It was the year after we had won the national championship. Three of our most senior defensive linemen had graduated after playing together for over four years. I was one of the few seniors returning for the upcoming season.

In 2011, our defensive line had a chemistry that was hard to build overnight. There was something about the 8:00 p.m. off-season workouts that had brought us together as a unit. The Saturday morning runs and team breakfasts over the years had built a bond that carried over to the toughest of moments in a game. The ups and downs during the seasons and the adversity we faced together had built our identity as the hardest-working group. We had repped our playbook so many times over the four years that, by 2011, we were able to line up in different positions and knew exactly what each one of us was doing on every single play.

Yet in that same *Hamilton Spectator* article, you would find my response to the concerns about our defensive line capabilities as: "I think the guys we have are pretty good. We'll be able to get the job done." How was I 100 percent confident in training camp that we were going to get the job done despite losing three starters? It's because we had depth. Our coaches had planned ahead.

First, our coaching staff had continued to recruit strong players over the years who had been training hard to step up. We had some strong first- and second-year players who were going to contribute massively. The coaches had made sure that the younger players got experience over the years. They always tried to get the junior players playing in games when we had a comfortable lead. This helped the young guys shake off the nerves and build confidence over the years.

Second, the coaches had a philosophy where we were always rotating the defensive line throughout the game. There would be eight of us during a game, and every other series some of us would rotate. We would rotate to keep us fresh. We would also rotate depending on the plays. Sometimes, I would come out of the game, and someone lighter and faster would go in during passing plays. Sometimes a lighter defensive end would come out, and a bigger defensive tackle would go in for short yardage plays. This meant that even the backups or specialists on the defensive line had accumulated significant experience over the past few years.

Lastly, we always played multiple positions. Our defense was built on a system versus relying on a single superstar. Which meant the coaches were able to shuffle around different players for different schemes. What made us unique was our ability to execute different schemes with the depth we had on the defense. We had some linebackers who would come up and play defensive end, and we would have some defensive ends who would drop in coverage. Even though we had a few gaps on the defensive line, we had enough versatility and skill set to fill these positions and play to the system.

So yes, our defensive line had taken a hit. But the group of guys stepping up was just as strong as the ones who had left. We were ready to get back after it. We continued our win streak that year with an 8–0 record. We made our way back to the national championship game for the second year in a row.

It was not a rebuild. It was a reload.

Concept:

When you're executing through multiple twists and turns and putting everything on the line, you will need all hands on deck. Depth is having the right team members who can step into the right roles and execute during critical times. Depth helps you fill any voids within the team to ensure business operations and execution don't suffer. Depth requires having a system where each role has a backup plan, and when the stakes are high, leaders are able to make progress and decisions with the right people.

With people changing jobs more frequently, and with the

environment that we operate in being unpredictable and uncertain, leaders must keep team depth top of mind. The notion of spending one's entire career at one company or in the same role is no longer the norm. A survey by Bankrate in 2021 suggested that 55 percent of Americans are likely to look for a new job in the next twelve months—also known as the Great Resignation. The average employee tenure at a company is four years. Millennials and Gen Zs expect to change jobs every two years.

Turnover is inevitable. Most employers need to be OK with that if they want to attract the best talent and build a great workplace culture. It's the reality that businesses need to work with. Unfortunately, it results in teams having key personnel changes every so often and leaders having to constantly hire and rebuild.

Having the right people who can take on a stretch role, step up, and also fill gaps in the team when needed can make the difference between winning a championship or not even making the playoffs. Most teams have a few star players. These are the players who drive your team forward. If a star player is no longer able to perform his or her role due to business or personal reasons, then having the proper depth will minimize the chaos and impact to your team's performance. Depth in this case is someone else on your team who can step into the existing role or someone external who can jump in quickly.

Having depth isn't about the size of your team or just cross-training someone for a different role. It comes down to having individuals who can execute in critical situations and make a difference, in case someone resigns unexpectedly or has a medical emergency, or because there are new, unanticipated business needs that need to be addressed. Depth requires planning and is methodical.

Another driver that makes depth a must in today's business environment is disruption. As disruption and competitive pressures continue to rise, businesses are having to respond faster and pivot more frequently. This means the amount of new projects, new initiatives, pivots, and changes are only going to increase, which will require teams and roles to shuffle constantly to best attack the demands of the future.

Side Note:

There were about three to four times a year when I was put on special projects. This was the same regardless of my role or title. That was the nature of the business—lots of new developments and opportunities requiring quick responses. The leadership team knew that it was the fastest and most effective to tap on individuals internally that can fill in the voids needed to tackle a high-priority, last-minute project. This results in constant reshuffling and realignment of key roles and individuals, which is only possible if you have enough depth in your teams.

Job descriptions are overrated.

Job descriptions are a big impediment to depth. Writing someone's duties and responsibilities on paper doesn't make sense anymore in an environment where the business unit, team, or the entire organization needs to shift every so often.

One of the primary reasons I was able to deliver results earlier in my career in heavy execution, pivot-based roles was because my job descriptions were flexible and dynamic. When I started out as a manager all the way through to director and then to VP of tech, I never saw a formal job description. Instead, I was always told about a problem I was hired to solve, what I had to deliver on, and what resources I could leverage to ensure I met my goal. Which meant finding ways to work with others, being resourceful, adapting, and getting creative. It was the best thing that could've happened to me because it allowed me to break down silos and do whatever was necessary to deliver on the results, which were always to the benefit of the organization. It taught me how to become resourceful and think like an entrepreneur.

For the same reason, I've never shared a job description with any of my team members. I stay away from a typical job description that has five or more sections loaded with tasks, duties, requirements, and allocates a time commitment percentage to each responsibility that seldom ever makes sense. That has never worked in my experience, especially when the rubber hits the road. Instead I shared a vision, expectations, and what results they would be responsible for. This means, at times, doing things that aren't necessarily in one's job description but that would help the collective team deliver on our mandate. It raised the level of accountability within the group.

Teams with great depth have individuals who understand the following:

1. Their key responsibilities
2. Their goals and deliverables
3. How they will work with others
4. How they will be evaluated
5. How their role helps the company achieve its overall objective

This provides individuals with what they need to deliver on and how to do it and promotes a more agile, nimbler behavior.

Sports to Business:

Football coaches prioritize depth. In fact, any coach in a team sports environment prioritizes depth. They recruit, train, practice, and to an extent even run the plays and schemes based on the depth they have. Come crunch time, every player on the team needs to be able to step into their role, even if it means playing a role that one isn't usually expected to play.

There are two areas in particular where coaches leverage depth to their advantage:

1. **Injuries during a Game**

   Unfortunately, injuries are a part of any sport, and coaches go into a game with a plan for injuries. Most positions have a designated backup. The starting player and backup practice interchangeably and take the reps needed during practice. It is all planned.

In addition to strong backups, the starting lineup also needs to know the basics of the position next to them on the field, court, or rink. This is critical in case an injury requires reshuffling the starting lineup. A football receiver needs to know the basics of other receivers, and at times the running back. For a middle linebacker, it means knowing how to sub in for the outside linebacker. And sometimes, for a defensive lineman, it means knowing how to play on the offensive line.

2. **Building for Next Year (Recruiting and Practicing)** This one's about having a long-term view and planning ahead. Who on the team can a coach groom into stepping up next year when a certain player leaves for another team or retires? This comes with giving the backup players the right coaching, development, and positive reinforcement needed so they are confident when it's time to step up next year. Sometimes a coach will play a rookie player when the team is winning, just to get him or her some game experience in a low-risk situation.

In terms of finding new players, great coaches are always recruiting and have a strong pipeline. In college it starts years before the high-school student graduates. Good schools identify young talent early and invest the time and effort to win them over.

In business, depth strengthens a leader's ability to address the following:

1. **Unexpected Changes**
   Great leaders recognize that they need team members who can play multiple positions. A business leader needs to have versatility and adaptability built into his or her team. When someone leaves the company, a project needs saving, or a team is battling a certain external threat, depth means having a few team members that you can plug into different positions.
   This is crucial for teams and organizations that are operating in super-fast-paced, high-pressure environments. For example, imagine you own a restaurant that is usually the busiest over the weekend. Now, if your chef calls in sick Friday night, what would you do? You can't shut the restaurant down or tell the customers to come back tomorrow. A great restaurant owner might have someone on call or someone in the staff trained to play the role of a chef for the night (enough to get by for the night). This same concept applies to a company with $100 million in revenues or $1 billion in revenues. The show must go on.

2. **Future Needs**
   Turnover is inevitable. Depth is also having a pipeline of strong individuals who can step into a role in the near future. This list can be either internal or external. A good

leader will always have a list of candidates who can take on a new role and keep the machine running smoothly.

A great leader also constantly recruits potential individuals to be ready for when the need arises. He or she views this as a core element of their role, with high return on their investment in the future. For example, imagine spending two hours a month on an ongoing basis connecting with potential candidates who can step into your key roles. When the need arises, you'll have someone in your pipeline who can jump into a role during your most critical moments. The return that these two hours a month generate is incomparable to any other form of recruiting.

3. **Balance**

Great depth provides a team much-needed balance. It helps balance the ups and downs and gives individuals the time needed to recover from hefty projects.

There are many people who have told me that it's not possible to be completely "off" and unplug on vacation. They say their job is too important, their boss needs them, or they are an integral part of the team. To all these excuses, I bring up lack of preparation and depth as the root cause. It is absolutely possible to unplug on your free time, if the individual and the leader of the team put in place the right structure and prepare for it as a priority.

If you have someone trained to cover your position, there are clear instructions and documentation on mission critical items, and if your time off is planned ahead of time, with the right communication to the right teams that depend on you, taking a true vacation is absolutely achievable. Again, it goes back to section 1 of this book, which is building the right foundations first. With the right foundations, it becomes easier to find balance during crazy times.

Action Plan:

This six-step plan will help you build and deepen your depth chart and position it as a core advantage.

Prep Step: Preassessment

1. Write down the names of all your team members in no particular order. Whether you're leading a team of executives, a department, or a cross-functional project team, in very few words, write down their key responsibility or areas they oversee below each name.
2. Now, under each name and role, write down who your number one backup is for that position in case the current team member was to leave today. Only put down a backup if that person can take on the new role and execute on 80 percent of the requirements of the role, as of today. It's OK to add the same person as backup to two positions. The idea is to see whether your current team can hold down the fort and execute without taking any major losses.

3. Does everyone on your team have a backup? If yes, then you're in good shape. If there are gaps, which we usually see for highly specialized, skilled positions, then you need to work on deepening your depth chart.

Step 1: Draw Your Depth Chart

Every team leader needs to have a depth chart. In business, we have all heard about our "org" chart—where you have a bunch of boxes set up in a hierarchy to show who occupies what role and the reporting structure. Similarly, it's of equal, and at times of higher, importance to build yourself a depth chart.

This is where, on a whiteboard or a PowerPoint slide, you list all of your current roles without a hierarchy. Instead, you group them by the primary objective for a set of roles in the case you have a large team. Otherwise, you can simply list them in any order.

Under each role title, write down a few words that describe the most critical function or responsibility of this position. For example, if you have someone who is a marketing manager, then you may write "oversee marketing calendar and execution." Or if you have someone who is the CFO, then write "financial oversight and strategic positioning of the business."

In football, a depth chart includes a snapshot of all the eleven (American football) or twelve (Canadian football) positions on offense, defense, and special teams. For example, on offense it will have the QB, running back, wide receivers, offensive linemen, and the tight end.

Once you've built out your roles, now list the names of the individuals that are in these roles. This will be your level-one plan.

Step 2: Build Your Two-Level Plan

Once you've finished your depth chart from step 1, identify the backups you need for each of the roles.

In your depth chart, under each of the roles and the individuals that occupy the role, write down at least one additional person on your team who can step into the role and deliver. You can have a certain team member be a backup for more than one position—that's totally fine.

The key is to determine who has the right skill set but also the adaptability to step into a role that is either different or a step up from his or her current role. This involves a bit of critical thinking on the leader's part but also some art and some faith.

As I was finalizing this book, the Toronto Maple Leafs and Montreal Canadiens were playing in the first round of the 2021 NHL playoffs. And in the first game of the series, John Tavares, Toronto's captain, got hit on a play and was taken out on a stretcher. He would end up missing the entire series.

After the game, Toronto's head coach made a statement: "It's a big loss for us, but we've got lots of depth. Good teams overcome these types of things. That's going to be on us."

Although Toronto lost to Montreal in that round in the final game of the series, it goes to show that you have to be ready to continue during the toughest moments. When a star player goes down at a crucial moment, you have to be able to continue without them.

You need to have someone ready who can step up or take on a different role. It's all a part of the planning. Great leaders always prioritize depth in their teams. As hard as it may be emotionally, plan for every situation and execute.

Step 3: Plan Your Successors

Now it's time to identify the "rookies" or members of the team who you want to train and get ready to step into key roles in the future.

Start by looking at the individuals who have the transferable skill sets to step into your key roles. Look at the three things one needs to perform in a particular role. For example, if one of your positions is a people partner, a role that aligns business objectives with people solutions and works with individuals to maximize success, then the key skill sets required for this role might be (1) communication, (2) strategic direction, and (3) influence and negotiation.

You can also identify individuals who are directly reporting to someone but have yet to mature from a management and team leadership standpoint. In these situations the focus would be on identifying who has the leadership traits to step into a role. In my experience the higher up I moved in a company, the more soft skills I needed to tap into.

Therefore, start identifying people in your team who either have a raw form of these traits or people who you believe can develop these with some training.

Step 4: Train for Multiple Positions

Build a plan to train everyone on your team for the positions identified in step 3. Similar to a sports season, this happens through ongoing practice, repetition, and live experience. It's important to groom these people to play the positions to which you've added them as backups.

Train your team to be able to step into these roles and hold down the fort when needed. Find ways to get someone time performing a few tasks that may be risk-free, or pair someone up on a project that will show them what the potential role looks like.

Across all of my teams, we always ensured someone could step into a different role and move things along. Which meant getting trained across different areas of the team. Some of these were roles that would be a natural progression, and some were roles that had a similar foundational skill set but different outputs.

When we didn't have the movement we needed on a project, someone was able to step up. When we had to fix data issues that affected over 50 percent of the business, someone was able to step up. And when a brand-new product launch didn't go as planned, the entire team was able to step up and get it done.

It also allowed us to cover for each other when on vacation. We had a rule that when someone is off, they are actually "off." Which means no emails, phone calls, or any other communication unless it was mission critical (which is rarely ever the case). We were able to stick to that rule because we had depth. And when I was away, I had team members step up, and I was fortunate to have the support of my colleagues from other departments who would step in. It was like clockwork.

Step 5: Train for Scenarios

Once you've got your whiteboard depth chart ready with your backups and successors, now it's time for the team to practice and get comfortable with the potential change as a whole. It's important to practice or come as close to a real-life situation where the team members need to take on a different role or step into a bigger role.

As a team, spend time doing a scenario exercise. Think of it as a simulation where you throw potential wrinkles in your strategy and go through the plan of attack with your team. Questions that need to be addressed include: What will the new priorities become? Who will need to step into different roles? Who will need to take on a completely different role? What skill sets will we need to acquire? And what data will you need to continue the positive momentum?

This will get your entire team thinking about how to execute with change and what everyone's role will be.

The day before our football game, we would do a drill where the starting twenty-four offensive and defensive players would stand in their respective positions on the field. Everyone else would be lined up on the sidelines. One by one, the coach would start calling out the names of the players on the field to simulate an injury. The name called would have to come off the field, and their backup from the sideline would have to jog onto the field and replace them. This drill was run at a fairly high speed and required clean, swift, clockwork-like substitutions. Very rarely would we have two people jog onto the field to replace the same person coming off the field, but if it did happen, that was the perfect time to clear things up, so it didn't happen come game day.

Step 6: Build Your Pipeline

Sometimes we don't have the right people available internally. There may be a certain skill set that just cannot be cross-trained, or there may be no one available to help you find depth in a critical moment. To expand on this idea, imagine being in the middle of a critical launch, and your star player has to leave the job for personal reasons. You cannot spend a week building out a job description, another week to sift through applications, and then another two weeks interviewing candidates. That is too slow in today's world. Therefore, it's very important, and the responsibility of every leader, not the HR team, to always be building your pipeline of potential external recruits that can step into your most critical roles.

I always say yes to a coffee chat with a graduating student or to a virtual connection with someone who reaches out and holds a similar role to what I have on the team currently. It does not take much effort but allows you to "interview" prospective recruits before you ever need them. I have personally received great ROI on such connections. For instance, during a particularly critical time, one of my key team members received an offer he could not refuse and decided to leave the team. It was not a role I could fill internally, given the specific skill set required. My depth chart could have someone step in for a few days or a week, but any longer and it would have affected our performance.

As it so happens, I had connected with someone who had reached out a few months earlier and kept them in my pipeline. So when my star player had to leave a few months before a major deadline, I hired his replacement within one week of his resignation. His ample notice and willingness to make it a smooth transition gave us two weeks of overlap time between him and his replacement. It made a world of difference given the tight timelines we were up against.

Always try to connect with at least a couple of potential candidates a month over a fifteen-minute coffee chat. It's less stressful than an interview for the candidate, and you get to see their human side while building your pipeline.

Side Note:

I've always believed that a leader is measured by the impact that they have on the individuals they lead. A manager needs to operate with the mindset of improving each and every individual's skill set and performance under their leadership. A measure of great leadership is the number of direct reports who got promoted, received competitive offers, or improved their annual performance scores.

If a key member of your team decides to leave for an opportunity of a lifetime, be happy for them. A leader should never hold others back or take it personally. It should be a proud moment for you, and you should celebrate the fact that you were able to positively contribute to their success. I was fortunate to report to leaders who understood this principle. Most leaders I reported to, always tried to elevate my performance, put me in positions to make big plays, and never held me back from pursuing my dreams, whether at the company or elsewhere. Empower and enable your people to make big plays.

Exercise:

- Why is it important to build your depth chart in business? In your depth chart, what are some immediate gaps that you need to address?

  ____

  ____

  ____

- How can you shift your job descriptions to become more results- and deliverables-based?

  ____

  ____

  ____

- If two of your star players, direct reports, or key individuals in a project or support role were to leave today, how fast would you be able to find their replacements? Do you have someone in mind, whether internal or external, or would it take you more than two weeks to post a new job opening and start the interviews?

  ____

  ____

  ____

- What are some things that you can implement in your team today to enable yourself to take vacation time, unplugged and guilt-free?

  ____

  ____

  ____

CHAPTER 14

Show the Promised Lands—Impact and Influence

If It Was Easy, Everyone Would Do It

In 2011, we were on a seven-game win streak after having lost the second game of the season 48–21 at home to the number one team in the conference, the Western Mustangs.

As the second ranked team, we were now competing for the Ontario University Athletics Conference championship, the Yates Cup, for the first time since 2003. But we were going up against the only team that beat us during the season—the Western Mustangs. We did not like Western. There are rivalries, and then there are *rivalries*.

We knew it was going to be a tough game. But we also knew we had come a long way since that loss earlier in the season. We had worked on all the things that went wrong in that game. We had consistently gotten better each week. We were confident heading into the game. The earlier loss was a distant memory that we didn't believe defined us as a team.

However, none of us on the team had ever gone to the conference finals. The last time McMaster beat Western was in 2007. Even with our win streak and the consistent growth week over week, there was still a bit of nervousness. We knew it wasn't going to be easy to go into a packed stadium away from home and face the top-ranked team.

The day before the game, we had our on-field pregame walk-through. At the end of the walk-through, our head coach was addressing the team before we left for the day.

Coach Ptaszek had won a Yates Cup during his college football days. He had been there. He knew what it took to get there and what winning the Yates Cup meant. He knew the doubts and nervousness that one felt before a big game. He also knew what it felt like playing against someone you've never defeated before. Above all, he knew what it felt like to win.

We were all on a knee in the huddle, and Coach P shared a few words to close off a strong week of practice. He didn't say anything about the game. He didn't say anything about the opponent. He didn't try to motivate us through a pep talk. Instead he smiled, and in an exciting, confident voice, said: "Yates Cup—that trophy is one of the heaviest trophies in football. When you lift it up, you can smell that over a hundred-year-old wood...one of the oldest trophies in Canadian football. When you hold it over your head...it's a special feeling. Can you imagine how great it's going to feel when we lift that trophy at Western? It's time to bring the Yates back home."

Coach P helped us see beyond what we had already accomplished. He showed us the promised land.

And we brought the Yates Cup back home with a 41–28 victory.

Concept:

When you've been working tirelessly for months, through many ups and downs, you might need that extra push to get your team through the finish line. A promised land combines motivation, influence, and impact as a leader in an uncertain, changing, or chaotic environment to propel the team forward, especially during the last push. A leader must show the team the destination—the prize that is waiting for them on the other side of this hard, obstacle-filled journey. By doing so a leader removes any doubts that the result is actually worth the sacrifices and hard work.

Good things take time. Long journeys get tiring and, at times, boring. No company becomes successful overnight. From fast-growing start-ups to companies undergoing large transformations, it takes hard work and dedication. These long journeys require you to give, give, and give before you can reap the rewards. They come with their fair share of setbacks. When you don't see results, you start doubting whether it's even worth it.

During those moments, quitting or giving up starts to become an option. And that is when seeing your promised land becomes so important. Your promised land becomes the extra bit of fuel, willpower, and resilience that you need when your back is up against the wall and everything is going wrong; it acts as the voice in your head that pushes you to do whatever it takes to get it done.

Leveraging your promised land is contingent on two factors. First, you need to be able to visualize your promised land. You have to see not just the light at the end of the tunnel, but what is waiting for you on the other side of the tunnel. In a business setting, this can be the recognition at the end of a successful project launch, it can be your well-deserved promotion after a year of hard work, or it can be your dream car that you really want to buy after hitting your sales targets. It can also be intrinsic, such as the feeling of proving others wrong who didn't believe you could achieve the impossible. When you can clearly visualize the promised land, it overpowers any pain, hardship, or obstacles in your way.

Second, the promised land that you visualize needs to be associated with a positive ROI. Whatever is waiting for you on the other side needs to be worth the cost. Whether it's the monetary investment you put into building a business, the extra hours you spend on evenings and weekends working toward your goal, or mental toughness you deploy in extremely chaotic environments, the reward has to be worth this cost. Furthermore, for a leader, the return has to be worth it to your entire team. Everyone must feel good about it as a collective unit. It can't just appeal to a few individuals—the entire team needs to believe in it.

Think about the last time when you personally worked day

and night to push through the final stages of a project without any additional monetary reward. Or the last time your team stepped up during the week of an important launch and worked through the entire weekend to get it done, despite any recognition or acknowledgment. Nine out of ten times it's because you and your team believed that the effort was worth the reward. Whether it was not letting your teammates down, proving a point, or setting yourself up for a promotion—you saw the promised land. Although monetary rewards motivate some people, it's always something bigger than a paycheck for most.

When everyone sees the promised land, understands how to get there, and can picture what winning feels like, it becomes a lot easier to push through moments of hardship and adversity. You're able to achieve more with less. You become more focused. You're able to step up your execution. You're able to block out all the noise. You're able to persevere through the ups and downs. And you're able to operate with resiliency.

Sports to Business:

Coaches ensure that the players see the "why" behind what they're doing. Gone are the days where a coach would make a team run laps around the field without any clear explanation. Great coaches today are methodical, and many have traded the authoritative push for bringing the athletes along on the journey.

Every year, every team, every coach, every player, regardless of the level of play, starts off with the goal to win the championship. Everyone puts in the work during off-season workouts, training camp, and throughout the season. But the teams that continue to push day in and day out are the ones that can visualize themselves holding that trophy.

In sports, a promised land allows you to do the following:

1. **See Past the Pain**
   Athletes always see past the back-to-back off-season workouts, twelve-hour training camp days, and long practices. They believe that the prize is worth all the pain.

2. **See Past Adversity as a Team**
   When a team is losing at halftime against the top-ranked team, or when things just don't go as planned—seeing the promised land allows teams to dig in their heels when their back is against the wall.

3. **See Past Tough Moments as Individuals**
   Unfavorable events are inevitable—a missed catch, a season-ending injury, or getting cut from the team at the end of training camp. What keeps strong athletes going back for more is never losing sight of their promised lands.

In a business environment, we do our best work when we feel fulfilled with a strong sense of purpose. It's a leader's responsibility to ensure the team can see the promised land.

Specifically, this means:

1. **Seeing Past the Pain**
   In business, a promised land allows teams and leaders to see past the mental exhaustion in business. Leaders see past the long hours with minimal return, see past the times of hardship, and see past the things they need to deliver that they might not be passionate about.

2. **Seeing Past Adversity as a Team**
   Similar to sports, shit happens. When a team has to deal with issues outside of their control, someone throws your team under the bus, or things blow up at the final stages of a project, seeing the promised land allows you to hunker down, focus on the big picture, and do the only thing that matters: execute.

3. **Seeing Past Tough Moments as Individuals**
   There are things that you can't control in business. A board member derails your pitch, someone passes you up for a promotion, or your top employee leaves. Great leaders find a way to get through these tough moments; promised lands help them get back to execution.

Action Plan:

Showing the promised land is less about getting buy-in or alignment from your team, which we discussed in the first section of this book. Rather, it's about motivating and lifting your team to push through the challenges and obstacles standing in your way—during that final push.

Here is a five-step plan that you can implement to have your team push through trying times when most teams may feel like giving up.

Step 1: Find Your Promised Land

As an individual, you need to first believe in and see your promised land with 100 percent clarity before you can motivate and influence others. If you personally don't believe that there is a light at the end of the tunnel or that winning is possible, then the team will see right through it. It's imperative that as an individual contributor, a team leader, a CEO, or whatever role you're playing, that you always have a clear vision of what lies beyond the tall, scary mountains standing in your way. It has to become the driving force behind all that you do.

Finding your promised land is about the shining star that everyone on your team shows up to work for.

Ask yourself, why do you do what you do? Why do you spend extra hours at work trying to solve a problem that you didn't create? Why does your team battle through failures and put in the work during the weekends without direct monetary reward?

Is it because you want to be known as the team that did it?

Is it about going down in history as the group of people that turned the business around?

Is it about fulfilling a promise that everyone made to each other before embarking on this project?

Find out what the end of the journey looks like. Find out

what the main reason is for your team to be here, and write it down.

Then find the promised land for your team. This is not to be confused with your top-level goals of growing revenues by 5 percent, for example, or entering a new market. Those goals are great for aligning your execution, but teams that work daily through the grind seldom ever see that as a motivational factor. Even if someone's bonus is tied directly to the financial outcomes, the reason many push through is most often something more intrinsic.

Step 2: Communicate the Feeling

Once you find the underlying motivation and what that trophy looks (and smells) like, make it known. Share it with your entire team, whether it's your direct team or your cross-functional team. Take a moment at the beginning of a huddle or your weekly Zoom all-hands meeting to take a step back and communicate what the promised lands are. You don't have to be leading a team to do this. Great leaders impact everyone around them in a positive way, regardless of rank or title.

Treat this as motivating and enabling your team versus simply stating your vision. Make the impact that you can on your team by describing the hidden treasure that awaits everyone.

One thing that I've seen great leaders do in sports and in business is storytelling. Why? Because we as humans are motivated by how we feel versus what someone tells us to do. In other words, you need to inspire your team versus presenting slide decks on where you're headed.

We need to communicate the feeling. This is the time to be passionate about your "why" as a leader. Be authentic. And any time you start a team meeting or a big regroup, always remind the team about why they do what they do. We've seen this concept in countless movies—it's the speech before a big game that makes all the difference. Small injections of passion can turn up the intensity of your team like never before.

There is a misconception that throwing a bunch of goals and targets on slides acts as motivation for your team. Goals, figures, data, and charts are great when aligning action plans and ownership, but they are not a substitute for motivation. Promised lands instead are associated with a feeling beyond facts, goals, or monetary compensation. Showing the promised lands must come from the heart. It's about finding what motivates your team at an intrinsic level and communicating it through a feeling. What always works is telling a story from the heart.

Step 3: Show Vulnerability and Authenticity

Twenty years ago this may have been something that many leadership gurus did not agree with. But in today's world, it would be a false sense of pride if a leader thinks he or she knows everything and needs to keep a fake persona between themselves and their team.

This does not mean that as a leader you wear your emotions on your face all the time. That can have devastating impacts. You don't want to show fear or lash out at someone on a call, especially when your team needs to find strength and courage during a tough stretch.

Showing vulnerability simply means communicating to your team that you're in this together. Share with your team that you may not have all the answers but as a team you will figure them out. Communicate to your team that it's not going to be easy, but at the same time show confidence and belief in your unit.

Vulnerability has two benefits. First, it shows your team that you're in the same boat as them, which strengthens the underlying motivation of pushing through together. And second, it helps you connect at a human level, which is something we tend to overlook in corporate environments today.

Step 4: Bring Others Along

Of course, not everyone will believe in your promised lands, especially if you need the help of peers or teams not in your group. It's even harder to get those who have zero vested interest in your work to push through and help you.

If a leader does his or her job well and aligns the entire organization on a handful of priorities as discussed in earlier chapters, there should never be a reason why one team would not want to support another. But during large transformations and as businesses adapt and change their business models, silos occur.

So identify the key stakeholders that must see and believe in your promised lands and find a way to get them on your team. Sometimes it takes a simple one-to-one conversation, and sometimes it's doing something above and beyond for a certain team or member. However you do it, always remember the why behind what you're doing, and that there is a common goal bigger than personal agendas or egos.

When you're in a position of authority but leading people who may be more experienced than you or leading a team that doesn't report to you, your success comes down to two things:

1. Earning their respect as we discussed in chapter 3
2. Showing the ROI of their time and effort

Therefore, like Dale Carnegie said, talk in terms of the goals, the benefits, and the interests of others. Along the way, showing that you truly care for others goes far.

Step 5: Send Constant Reminders

Unless you enjoy the journey, the promised land doesn't mean much. Remember, the return needs to be worth the effort. Enjoying your journey reduces the cost and increases your likelihood to see things through.

You have probably seen big speeches from leaders or coaches before a big game. What we usually don't see is that they never stop communicating the promised land behind the scenes during the unseen hours. During tough workouts, during a tough loss, during a bad call in a game, coaches are always communicating. They remind the team why everyone chose to be on the field at seven in the morning on a Saturday when their friends were sleeping in. They make the journey more bearable.

Similar to some previous chapters, a healthy dose of "why it all matters" is important. You can get away without overly communicating when things are running smoothly. But when you're in the playoffs and things take a wrong turn, great leaders never stop communicating and reminding the team about the "why." This is where great leaders make their impact. During times of hardships, uncertainty, and chaos, remind your team again and again at any chance you get. Overcommunicate. It's never enough.

The same goes for you at an individual level. Always keep reminding yourself about your promised land. If you have to write quotes on your whiteboard, do it. If you have to set calendar reminders to visualize your promised land, do it. Constantly remind yourself why it's all worth it.

Exercise:

Here are a few questions that can help you get started in finding your promised land:

- What is your personal promised land?

  ____

  ____

  ____

- How can you communicate your promised land to your team? What are some ways you can maximize the impact you have on your team in a positive way?

____

____

____

- How can you bring others along the journey who don't necessarily report to you? Think back to some scenarios you've encountered. What can you do differently?

____

____

____

CHAPTER 15

Be Proud, but Never Satisfied

You're Never as Good, or as Bad, as You Think

There is one morning in particular that I remember from the football days. We were ranked fourth in the country and were slated to be a contender for the conference championship (Yates Cup). Other than an early season loss to Western, we had plowed through every other team and were likely on our way to the playoffs.

After winning one of our regular-season games in the second half of the season, we were on the field at eight the next morning for our team rundown. Some jogging and stretching would help remove postgame soreness and speed up recovery.

That morning we went through our regular run down and were getting ready to stretch and cool down on the field. But just before we got into our stretch lines, Coach Ptaszek asked everyone to huddle up.

He said, "If we're to become the best team in the nation, we can't be taking penalties." Now I don't remember how many penalties we'd taken, but we were one of the most penalized teams that week.

Then he said, "Everyone—line up across the goal line. We're going to jog it to the other end zone and back. Every ten-yard line, we're doing five push-ups, all the way there and back."

There weren't too many happy faces. Especially us linemen. We ran enough during the game and in the rundown. We didn't want to run any more. It seemed almost unnecessary at first. We had won the game. We were sore. We were hurt. We needed to recover instead of sprinting and doing over one hundred push-ups. This seemed counterintuitive to all the strength and conditioning principles we'd been taught over the years. We should be sitting down watching game film with ice packs on our bruises and injuries.

Coach P said, "Go," and we jogged over to the goal line to get into position, forming a single line from sideline to sideline. We got into position for Coach P to blow the whistle. But there was no whistle. Instead, Coach P jogged over and made his way to the center of the goal line, beneath the goal post. Then he raised his hand and said, "we're doing them together, on my count."

He was going to do it with us. And that changed everything. All of a sudden, it became a lot bigger than just a coach punishing his team for taking too many penalties. It became about being disciplined as a team, it became about accountability as players *and* coaches, and above all, it became about never being satisfied as a team. It became about pursuing excellence with high standards, and something that was much greater than any one person on that field. It became about winning as one unit, one family.

Even though we had won the game, we could not be content with how we played if we wanted to compete with the teams outside of our conference. We could not be satisfied.

With Coach P leading, eighty or so Marauders ran down the field, doing push-ups at every ten-yard line, all the way down to the other end zone and back. When we got back, we huddled in the end zone to break it down. This huddle was different. I don't remember what Coach P said, and I don't think he said much at all. But I'm 100 percent certain that each one of us remembers that feeling. It was an understanding that being good isn't good enough and a commitment that said, "I won't let my teammates down when it matters the most."

Coach P could have just made us run, or he could've just addressed the penalties in the film session. But looking back, if we hadn't done those push-ups, maybe some of the stories in this book might not exist.

As I said in the opening chapter of this book, it starts with leadership. It starts with taking action against mediocrity. It starts with setting high standards. It starts with you.

Concept:

Once you've made some big plays and delivered on key milestones, the journey doesn't end; you need to prepare to come back stronger. Being proud but never satisfied is an attitude. It's a mentality where you always strive to do better. It doesn't mean you don't enjoy your accomplishments or don't celebrate. I wrote a whole chapter about celebration in this book because it's an absolute must. But never being satisfied is about celebrating your accomplishments *and* continuing to grow. They go hand in hand.

Our defensive line coach, Carm Genovese, would often say "You're never as good, or as bad, as you think." This attitude puts you in positions to capitalize on big opportunities. It's a relentless drive to constantly improve, get better, and outdo yourself every single day. You're always learning, growing, iterating, and adapting as part of the process. Over time it all adds up. To others your success will seem like a lucky stroke. But when you look back, you can trace your success back to the work you put in every single day, even on the days you didn't feel like getting out of bed.

Never being satisfied is important in business, in sports, and in life. It is actually one of the best defenses against complacency. Complacency has killed thousands of great businesses and careers (corporate and pro sports). Complacency is particularly harmful during the postseason—when we've seen some early success and convinced ourselves that we're good enough. It is even more harmful during the off-season after we've won. While we can get immediate negative feedback for complacency during the playoffs by losing the game or failing to deliver results, there is minimal feedback during the off-season. By the time you see the warning signs, it may be too late, and you might be headed well into the execution mode. So you must continue to improve and hold yourself accountable, especially when no one's watching.

We've discussed how digital disruption has resulted in numerous businesses going from billions in market capitalization to bankrupt over the past twenty to thirty years. New technology and tech-first entrants have disrupted long-standing traditional businesses. But disruption is never the culprit. It all boils down to being complacent in the face of disruption.

In recent history, most of the time it was either because of one of the following:

1. The company or leadership didn't believe that new emerging companies and start-ups were a threat and did not respect their competition and therefore did not innovate fast enough, or
2. The companies and leadership were too fixated on their existing business models and solutions and discredited where consumers were going.

Both of these are driven by a lack of respect to where the macro environment, customers, and business in general are going. Great sports coaches never underestimate their opponents. They respect their competition. They could be facing an undefeated team or a team that hasn't won a single game. The level of preparation for both is the exact same. Great coaches know that teams that haven't won a single game are the hungriest and the most dangerous. The same applies to business and emerging start-ups today. Great organizations respect their competition and innovate like their life depends on it, regardless of the level of past success.

Our ability to adapt to new threats is a lot better when we're continuously seeking out new strategies and innovations in order to continue to get better versus waiting until we're caught like a deer in the headlights. In other words we find success and continue to achieve more when we respect our competition and are not complacent.

As an individual example, consider two recent grads who have just entered the workforce. They both started as analysts at the same company. One of the grads, Tom, sees this new role as a great accomplishment and is happy with the work he's doing. He's content with the role and the responsibility he is given. The other grad, Stacey, also sees this role as a great accomplishment in her young career but believes she can achieve more. A lot more. She aspires to be a director in the company within the next five years. Who do you think is at a higher risk of being disrupted by things outside of their control?

It's Tom. Because he's satisfied, he will likely exhibit less proactive behavior in improving himself to remain competitive. Stacy, on the other hand, will naturally gravitate toward taking actions that bring her closer to her goal, such as networking, professional development, and taking on stretch roles. Her never-satisfied attitude will always propel her to keep her head on a swivel, building the skill sets she needs to thrive in the future.

No industry, business, technological innovation, or circumstance is ever the reason behind a lack of career growth. It's usually an individual's lack of hunger and drive. When you get comfortable, you get complacent. That is exactly when you need to find roles, projects, or situations to make yourself uncomfortable again.

Side Note:

In my final year of MBA, I had already accepted a job offer for a role that was starting the summer after graduation. When selecting courses for my final semester, I found a course offering that required students to consult for a multinational company during a four-month project. We had to apply to be selected for the course, and it was known to come with a heavy workload: about thirty hours a week in addition to four other classes. Looking at the workload and the fact that I already had a full-time role lined up, I decided not to apply.

I remember talking to my wife (then girlfriend) about it. She said, "The reason for taking courses is to learn, not to take the easy road for a high GPA. Besides, your goal for your MBA was never to get a job. It was to learn and acquire the tools and networks necessary for life." Long story short, I applied and got selected. The client I worked with during that course was the company that hired me two years later after I switched career paths. This was the company where I started my tech journey as a manager with no prior tech experience and was promoted three times in three years. Had I not taken the course, I wouldn't have written this book. My wife reminded me not to be complacent. You must always be striving for more.

Sports to Business:

In sports, you cannot be at the top of your game, no matter what sport it is, and not have a target on your back. The better you become, the harder someone else is working to try and take your spot.

This is true in tennis for someone who's ranked top ten. This is true in high-school soccer for the starting striker. This is true in the NFL for a five-year starting linebacker. This is also true for the best team in the league. Everyone is gunning to beat the best team at the top.

In sports, being proud but never being satisfied comes down to the following:

1. **Having an Underdog Mentality**
   Teams and athletes are the most dangerous when others discount them and don't see them as a threat. Great athletes use the lack of respect as motivation and fuel. It's a mindset that helps them stay hungry. It becomes a force that pushes athletes to put in the work to prove everyone wrong. It gives teams a chip on their shoulders.

2. **Finding Perspective**
   Regardless of how many games a team wins, there's always more. They always find something to improve upon even after a win. Whether it's going further in the

playoffs, continuing the win streak, or winning back-to-back championships, great teams always strive for more. If Tom Brady had been content after winning two Super Bowls, he wouldn't be known as the GOAT today.

3. **Leading by Example**
   Great athletes lead by example. They show up early to practice, are critical of their performance during film review, and are back at the gym the morning after the game. This kind of work ethic is contagious. It starts with the leaders of the group.

In business, not being satisfied translates to the following:

1. **Having an Underdog Mentality**
   At an organization and individual level, this mindset tackles complacency. Because businesses are getting disrupted and many career skill sets are becoming commoditized, having an underdog mentality leads you to consistently find new opportunities for growth. Champions always keep their head on a swivel. They execute with the mentality that someone else is coming for their job.

   I always think back to some of the interviews featuring The Rock—Dwayne Johnson. He mentioned that in the mid '90s, he was cut from the CFL (Calgary Stampeders) and went back home to Tampa Bay with just seven dollars in his pocket. What drove him to succeed were these hard times. In 2021, when he was worth millions of dollars and the highest-paid actor according to *Forbes*, he attributed his success to always remembering where he came from. Regardless of how successful he was, those hard times give him that motivation to continuously strive for greatness.

2. **Finding Perspective**

   Leaders never let an easy job, a great track record, or a strong market where delivering results are easy stop them from going above and beyond. They don't allow past years' performances to translate into a false sense of pride. They always take a step back and put things into perspective. Regardless of how great of a year you had, there is always someone who did it better. Seeing where you fit pushes you to become relentless and builds resilience. There's always more.

3. **Leading by Example**

   People follow the example of role models. A leader cannot expect greatness from their team if he or she does not walk the talk. A leader must continue setting the tone regardless of how far the team has come. A leader must always maintain high standards. Hard work and high standards are contagious, and these are the building blocks of a culture with relentless drive.

Action Plan:

Here is a four-step plan to build a mentality where you can feel proud, set high standards, and battle complacency.

Step 1: Recognize Your Accomplishments

As you achieve success and break through barriers, it's important to recognize how far you've come. Every six months, or sooner, if it makes sense, show your team what you as a unit were able to accomplish. Have concrete, quantitative metrics that you can share. This will help boost your team's confidence regardless of how the overall business did.

This is important because it shows you and the team that whatever you've done is working. It is getting results. And this is the time to feel proud of your accomplishments.

This is also when you should celebrate as discussed in chapter 10. When a sports team wins an important game, overthrows a strong rival, or wins the championship, they recognize their achievements. It's totally fine to feel proud of the hard work.

Many teams recognize great plays on a weekly basis, and almost all teams host their own year-end awards. Most major leagues have year-end all-star lists. It's all about recognizing the hard work you've done and the distance you've covered.

The point here is to show that where you ended is not where you started, and that is how you carry the momentum forward on a positive note.

Step 2: Zoom Out

As you feel proud of your accomplishments, the reality is that the better we get, the easier things get, and the easier the things get, the more complacent and satisfied we tend to become.

Therefore, it's equally important to take a step back and show your team and be honest with yourself on where you stand from a grand scheme of things. If you're a medium-sized company that just grew revenues by 100 percent, then where do you stack up against other companies within your industry? Make a list of all other medium-sized companies in your industry by overall market share and show where you are.

You'll notice one of three things:

1. You've graduated from your current level of competition (your league) and now are going up against the big dogs,
2. You have others that have also done equally well, or
3. You're the top dog, and now you have a target on your back.

Regardless of which one it is, it's a good reminder that there is more to do and more to accomplish. In fact, the better you become, the harder you have to work. Therefore, it's very important to balance point one above with this point.

I was the first one to attend university in my extended family. That was a great accomplishment that my parents were proud of. But once I got to university, there were thousands of other students who were now competing with me. So, sure

I was proud, but it wasn't much of an accomplishment once I zoomed out.

After a grand slam victory, Roger Federer celebrates, feels proud, and then simply continues to put in the work to prepare for the next tournament. After winning a Super Bowl, the Tampa Bay Buccaneers started preparing for the next season in a matter of weeks. There's always more that needs to be done. Elite athletes know that the only way to continue getting better is knowing that someone is always coming for their spot.

Step 3: Tap into the Underdog Mentality

Of course, it's a lot easier said than done. When you've won a championship or put up industry-leading results, it's a lot harder to keep innovating as you did when no one knew who you were. It's hard to repeat the level of success again when everyone is working hard to beat you.

It's even harder to continue putting in the work when you know you improved a lot over the year but haven't been recognized for that work by your boss or colleagues. That is when we tend to lose motivation. But that's also when we're the closest to a breakthrough.

That is why, regardless of how successful you get as an individual, team, or a company and regardless of the type of recognition you've received, the tenacity, sense of urgency, and focus must stay alive. You need to find a way to believe that you're still an underdog, and your only job is to prove the critics wrong.

As an individual contributor climbing that ladder, this is when you need to remember the hard times and continue striving for the top. All the concepts in this book will take you to a certain level of performance, but constantly striving to improve day over day, regardless of the circumstances, is what drives it home.

Step 4: Repeat, Repeat, Repeat

Lastly, it's all about growth. You can never stop growing. When you find success in the form of a big win, a new deal, a promotion, secured funding, or whatever else it may be, set that as your new baseline. That level of performance must now become what you compare yourself against, and you must only improve.

Analyze your success, celebrate, and readjust your plan. Increase your targets, build your foundations, execute, and find that momentum.

What worked for you before may not work for you in the future. If you keep the same level of execution, complacency will creep in, which will make you vulnerable to others who are hungrier.

My speed training coach, Andrew Yap, messaged me after many years when he saw that I had accepted the role of VP of tech for a publicly traded company. He said, "Keep moving forward and enjoying life. Be well and keep reaching for the top in your career." He did what a great coach always does—reminds his players that there is always more to accomplish. Keep going!

Be proud, but never satisfied. Keep going. That is the P.R.O. Business Mindset.

Exercise:

As the final exercise for the book, this one may take you outside of your comfort zone. Because that's where growth happens.

- Write down your top three priorities today. These can be personal, professional, or a mix of both.

  ____

  ____

  ____

- Give yourself a score of one to ten on your dedication and drive for each. One would be where you've neglected it completely, and ten would be where you've given it all you've got.

  ____

  ____

  ____

- For the priorities that you ranked below a ten, ask yourself the following:
    - What are you the most proud of? What have you done well consistently?
    - What areas are you lacking in? Have you become satisfied? Complacent?
    - What can you do today to increase that score, even if it's by one point?

Be as honest and open with yourself as you can be. The point is to be objective.

- Write down your answers and build your personal action plan to help you break through any complacency or barriers.

    ____

    ____

    ____

PART 2

Game Highlights

This section includes select one-on-one interview summaries with current and former elite-level athletes and coaches turned business leaders.

The roster includes athletes from the NFL, NHL, MLB and CFL, Olympians, NCAA student athletes, and coaches, among others. They have held executive and entrepreneurial roles at companies including Walmart, SkipTheDishes, RBI, Gold's Gym, Oracle, and DraftKings, among others.

Each summary includes a key message and a takeaway on leading, adapting, and winning in a world full of chaos, uncertainty, change, and digital disruption.

You can also watch the full interviews by visiting the *Sports to Business* podcast page below.

www.tanvirbhangoo.com/sports-to-business-podcast/.

FOR LEADERS

FOCUS ON THE FUNDAMENTALS

Bob Gibson
Chief Revenue Officer, Jolt; Former GVP, Oracle MICROS
Junior Football Coach, eighteen-plus years

I had the privilege of working with Bob on a few important projects, and I always admired his solution-oriented leadership style. During our chat, Bob mentioned that he had gone through three market crashes over the course of his career. I asked him about the X factor behind his success as an executive despite the ups and downs.

Bob said, "A big part of it is paying attention to the fundamentals. It's another analogy to sports...tackling and blocking is really important. It's not the fluff (that matters). I always like to say that the real work is done in the trenches. It's part of my DNA, building the foundations. And as you do that over time, over the course of your career...like building a great network, it pays dividends over time."

Concept

Teams that win championships first get the basics right. They don't rely on silver bullets, trick plays, or mere luck. Instead, great teams spend time practicing the fundamentals and getting really good at the basics. The fundamentals allow them to make big plays down the road.

Takeaway

Thriving in disruption and uncertainty requires a strong set of fundamental skills. You have to put in the time up front in order to take advantage of future opportunities. Whether it's practicing your presentation skills, building your network, or learning a new skill set every year, focusing on honing the basics will allow you to adjust and weather any storm with confidence.

ORDINARY PEOPLE WITH EXTRAORDINARY DREAMS

Devon Harris, OLY
Motivational Speaker
Olympian, Founding Member of the Jamaican Bobsled Team

I asked Devon how his Olympic journey started and the story behind the Jamaican Bobsled Team during the 1988 Winter Olympics. A story also depicted in the movie *Cool Runnings*, which is considered one of the best underdog movies of all time.

He said, "I am fifteen years old, running track, and training seriously for the first time. ABC Wide World of Sports had this series called *Road to Moscow*, as the Moscow Olympics were coming up the following year, in 1980. They featured athletes from around the world...talking about their lives...and the thing that struck me, Tanvir, was how average and ordinary they were."

The TV series opened a realm of possibilities for Devon. He saw that the Olympians were average people, just like everyone else. But what separated them was that they had extraordinary dreams, with equally extraordinary desires. Eight years later the Jamaican Bobsled Team made history.

Concept

No one is born an Olympian, and no business becomes a unicorn overnight. Everyone starts from ground zero. Some of the most successful athletes in the world of sports and Olympics were just regular people who came from humble beginnings. But they had larger-than-life goals and a drive to match those goals.

Takeaway

Building a new career, turning around a business, pulling a company out of decline, or simply finding work that is meaningful is absolutely possible. Devon's story is proof that regardless of our circumstances, if you dare to dream big enough, you can achieve the impossible.

RAISE YOUR HAND

Kelly MacPherson
Chief Technology and Supply Chain Officer, Union Square Hospitality Group
Former CIO, Restaurant Brands International (Burger King, Tim Hortons, Popeyes)

I asked Kelly what was behind her success as a technology executive. What allowed her to lead global tech strategy at billion dollar companies? She said earlier in her career she never sought out to be in technology. Coming from a family of entrepreneurs, Kelly's dad had her playing multiple roles, and that pushed her to tackle whatever the business demanded at the time. It taught her to always raise her hand and not be afraid of "falling forward."

When she started her career at Planet Hollywood as a restaurant manager, she accidentally landed in technology when the company needed someone to become a POS expert. Six weeks later she was on the road opening new restaurants. That led to executive positions at Hard Rock Cafe, Abercrombie & Fitch, and Restaurant Brands International.

Concept

Great athletes say yes when their name is called. They might have to play a different position, or sit on the bench, or carry the equipment out on the field before every practice. That flexible, open-minded attitude leads to great opportunities.

Takeaway

Effective leaders take initiative. Accelerate your performance by doing things that others don't want to do, during times of hardship or need. Doing so allows you to learn faster, build a track record, and, as seen in Kelly's case, build a niche skill set that becomes hard to replicate.

HUMILITY AND PERSEVERANCE

Devon McDonald
Partner, OpenView Venture Partners
NCAA DI Basketball Player

Former NCAA Division I Basketball Player Devon McDonald shared her story behind becoming a partner at OpenView, a venture capital fund with over a billion dollars of assets under management. Devon heard about OpenView in 2009 and decided that's where she wanted to work and build her career in VC (venture capital).

During her meeting with OpenView, she was so impressed with the vision and team that she said, "I'll take any job! What's available?" OpenView was looking to hire for a brand-new experimental role that would be focused on helping the portfolio companies scale their inside sales teams, a role that felt a little daunting and undefined initially. She said yes and took a leap of faith. Six years later, she became a partner at the firm.

I asked Devon what allowed her to carve her own path. She said her experience as an NCAA basketball player played a big part. A big part of her role at OpenView has been doing work behind the scenes. Playing roles as a student athlete that were not always in the spotlight helped her build the humility and perseverance needed to thrive in the business world.

Concept

Not everyone on the team gets their photo in the newspaper. Many players have to take on roles that aren't in the spotlight, such as playing a backup or being on the practice team. But they do so with humility and pride, because they recognize that they are one piece of a greater collective.

Takeaway

Devon's story is a great example of how humility drives ambition. Reaching the top takes hard work—work that doesn't always get recognized by those on the outside. Building a strong career through hard work starts with humility.

FOCUS OVER HARD WORK

Jeremiah Brown
Professional Keynote Speaker and Author, *The 4 Year Olympian*
Olympic Rower, Silver Medalist

Jeremiah, "The 4 Year Olympian," went from his couch to winning an Olympic medal in four years. I asked Jeremiah if hard work is the be-all and end-all. What he said next has had a big impact on how I approach execution today.

He said, "I feel like you've got to work hard, but focus is more important. Assuming the hard work is there, the focus is what's at risk these days...we're all inundated with all these possibilities, and opportunities, and what we could be doing. If I bring it back to keynote speaking, that's all I do. I'm working every day on my flagship keynote; I'm doing repetition. I'm bringing the athlete mindset to a very specific market. And great things will happen because you have the discipline and focus to see it through."

Concept

When we hear the word "athlete," what comes to mind? An individual that is solely focused on his or her craft. Athletes are focused on one sport, one position, and oftentimes known best for one or two things. For example, being a great three-point shooter, a one-hundred-meter sprinter, or one that almost everyone knows—Beckham's curved free kick (a.k.a. bend it like Beckham). Athletes focus on their craft and put all they have into their sport.

Takeaway

In a world full of disruption, it's important to focus on a few things and do them really well. It's about finding a niche and being completely obsessed. Whether it's an industry, a technical skill set, or a new market, understand the variables, understand the problem you're trying to solve, and be ruthlessly focused about solving it. Work on your craft. Stay focused.

MAKE YOUR OWN LUCK

Cedric Clark
VP Operations, Sam's Club (Walmart)
Former NCAA DI Basketball Player

Cedric played NCAA basketball for Washington State University. Cedric initially attended the University of Arizona. He said, "I showed up there and said, 'You know what? I'm going to try out and try to make the team.' I was one of two people who got the tryout, but I didn't make the team. Believe it or not, guess what the coach told me? He said, 'Hey, you should be a practice player for the women's team. That would be a good thing for you to do on your journey to making the team.'"

Cedric swallowed his pride and said yes. It taught him what it meant to be a student athlete, and even got him a courtside seat to the national championship game. At the end of that year, Cedric knew he'd have a better chance of making the University of Washington team. The coach at Arizona put in a good word for him, and Cedric just showed up to the preseason conditioning sessions at Washington. Cedric said, "No one said no, and I never looked back."

Concept

The great athletes we hear about have all gone through adversity and their own struggles. The best of the best were sometimes cut from the team, were never drafted, or were told they would never win. What differentiates athletes who have defied odds is their will to win and persevere.

Takeaway

It's easy for others to tell you that what you're trying to do is impossible. People may shoot down your start-up idea, say you're making a bad career move (I was told three times), or dissuade you from climbing that corporate ladder. But Cedric's story shows us that everything is possible if you are willing to make your own luck.

PRACTICE MAKES PERFECT

Courtney Stephen
Director, Community Partnerships, Hamilton Tiger-Cats Football (CFL)
Former CFL Player

Courtney and I played football together during our middle and high school years. He was drafted eighth overall in the CFL. During his pro football career, he was equally as dedicated to building his speaking and training business.

I asked Courtney what the biggest lesson he learned was in football that he applied to his business career. He said, "Certain things that you had to initially give a lot of effort to, for example, following up with somebody, being on time, or managing your schedule, the smallest of things, even just having a thirst to know more about a topic that you're going to have to speak to somebody about...these little habits, you do them so much over time that they become your second nature. Your default behaviors become your success habits."

Concept

Practice, practice, practice. Sports is all about practice. Elite athletes spend countless hours practicing the basic moves. No matter how successful they get, they continue practicing the basics. Practicing the little things day in and day out builds success habits. And these habits become the foundation for future growth.

Takeaway

Identifying the little things that one must do every day, and doing them consistently over time, becomes a superpower. Practicing your presentation skills, finding time to meditate, or blocking off time for quiet work are all examples of the little things that we can do day in and day out, repeatedly, to build on the basics. Over time, these become second nature, which allows you to focus on the higher-priority items.

BURN THE BOATS

Dan Hannigan-Daley
CEO, Sports Info Solutions
Former Canadian University Soccer and Hockey Player

Dan Hannigan-Daley heads up Sports Info Solutions (SIS), a sports data and analytics company with clients including ESPN, MLB, NFL, and NBA teams. When Dan left university, he had an internship opportunity locally in Toronto but decided to go overseas. He explained, "For whatever reason, I was like I have to get out of here. I want to go overseas, go to the UK, and witness life over there. This is an opportunity to see what happens."

Dan booked a one-way ticket to London and decided to make his own fate. He knocked on all the doors: English Premier League clubs, Scottish Premiership clubs, as well as clubs from smaller leagues. But he came up short. In the process, however, he came across an opportunity to attend the University of East London. That led to his first role with BD Sport Group. Fast-forward, that trajectory took him to DraftKings where he was a director before becoming the CEO at SIS.

Concept

Winning is never guaranteed. Only a small percentage of athletes win a championship. But no athlete will ever say they regretted their decision to go all out and give it their best. The long-term rewards of committing to a journey full of opportunities, memories, friends, and knowledge most often outweigh any short-term gains or failures.

Takeaway

We will only reach our potential when we fully commit. "Burning the boats" leaves us with no option of going back. Instead, it pushes us to find and knock on every single door that we see, as well as those we can't see. Have faith in your abilities, have the right attitude, and believe. Make that leap of faith. Commit.

WE FALL DOWN TO GET BACK UP

Jesse Lumsden
Partnerships Team Lead, Neo Financial
Three-Time Olympian and Former CFL Player

A McMaster football all-star running back and record holder, Jesse Lumsden is a name that every Canadian football fan knows. His story, though, is full of injuries. In 2008, he injured his shoulder playing for Hamilton (CFL), which needed surgery. He then returned to play with Edmonton the following season. In the first game of the season, he injured the same shoulder again, which needed another surgery.

In 2010, Lumsden transitioned to bobsled and participated at the 2010 Winter Olympics for Canada. After the Olympics, he returned to football and suffered yet another season-ending knee injury. Retiring from football in 2010, Lumsden focused solely on bobsled. At the 2014 Winter Olympics, after running the second-best time in the second heat in four-man bobsleigh, the sled crashed and flipped over on the next run. It was scary to watch.

I asked him, "How did you keep going? Many would've given up much earlier." He said, "What does Alfred say to Bruce Wayne when Batman falls down? Alfred says, 'Why do we fall, sir? So that we can learn to pick ourselves up.'" In Lumsden's case, getting back up was winning a Silver at the 2017 World Championships and finishing sixth at the 2018 Winter Olympics.

Concept

Falling down is inevitable. Injuries and losing are part of the game. At times, great athletes go through an unlucky string of injuries and losses. Yet the best athletes gather themselves and continue moving forward, because that is all they know.

Takeaway

Business is only getting tougher. With fierce competition and strategic plans changing every year, losing, failing, and at times getting the shorter end of the stick are part of the game. If there is one thing we can do during these moments to maximize our chances of success in the long term, it's getting back up and getting back after it.

COMPARTMENTALIZE YOUR PRIORITIES

Drew Taylor, PhD
CEO and Cofounder, Acorn Biolabs
Former Minor League Pitcher

Drew Taylor is cofounder and CEO of Acorn Biolabs, a Toronto-based health care technology company. Acorn has developed and patented novel mechanisms to collect, analyze, transport, and store live cells from individuals to use in regenerative medicine strategies. They offer the ability to cryogenically store these cells in advance, stopping the aging of these cells, and protecting them from cellular damage and degradation due to age and disease. In addition, Acorn offers live cell, genetic, and epigenetic analysis.

Drew played and served as team captain for the Michigan Wolverines during his undergraduate and master's degrees in molecular, cellular, and developmental biology. While playing professional baseball, Drew was a full-time PhD student at the University of Toronto Institute of Biomedical Engineering program. During our conversation he said, "There was one occasion where I wrote an exam in Toronto in the morning, and I was pitching in a small town outside of Chicago that evening."

When I asked Drew how he juggled being a PhD student and a professional baseball player at the same time, he said, "You're not going to be a very good pitcher if you're on the mound thinking about the exam the next day, and you're not going to be performing that exam to the best of your ability if you're thinking about what you need to do on the mound later that evening." It comes down to compartmentalizing key priorities, focusing on the task at hand.

Concept

A two-hour football practice is split up into predefined activities and drills. There are a set number of minutes allocated to warm-ups, positional drills, one-on-ones, team scrimmages, cooldowns, etc. Every player and every coach respects the time allotted to each activity and moves swiftly from one to the next. It's a great example of focusing on the task at hand without worrying about the upcoming drill or how you performed in the previous session.

Takeaway

Every year, the number of distractions and competing priorities in the business world are increasing. We need to do more with less. In a world full of options, identify a few key priorities and build a system to focus on the task at hand. Whatever you're doing, do it to the best of your ability while being present in the moment.

REST IS A WEAPON

TJ Galiardi
Cofounder and CMO, Outcast Foods
Former NHL Player

I was super excited to speak with TJ, one of the first NHL players to be on the podcast. TJ cofounded Outcast Foods, and in 2021 raised $10 million in initial funding. A very humble and down-to-earth athlete turned entrepreneur, I asked TJ how he found balance in his business and life.

He said, "I used to love the line 'rest is a weapon.' If there was ever an optional skate (in the NHL) or optional practice, I was taking it every time! You see a lot of executives that burn out... and I kind of felt it when I started with my business. It was on my mind every minute of every day. I would be in bed, and at three in the morning I'd wake up, and I'd be thinking about some minor thing. I had to train myself to get away from that because I knew it was going to burn me out."

So TJ made it a priority to find time every day to work out, to get away from his phone, and disconnect. Something he calls his "reset button."

Concept

We've seen numerous advances in technology that help athletes optimize rest and recovery for better performance. Rest is important with great research to back it up. The movies that show someone training hard every single day, or coaches running their team to the ground, actually have devastating effects on performance in reality.

Takeaway

Since moving to a remote/hybrid work environment with the COVID-19 pandemic, the hours worked, stress, and burnout have all increased. Businesses and leaders must find the right balance and prioritize rest and recovery as a fundamental part of their team's operations. The teams that can balance hard work with rest and recovery will go much further than those pushing with no gas in the tank.

BUILD YOUR TOOL BOX

Femi Ayanbadejo, MBA
Founder and CEO, HealthReel; NASA Tech Partner
Former NFL Player and Super Bowl Champion

I love Femi's drive for knowledge and his pursuit to acquire a diverse set of skills. After retiring from the NFL, he founded tech company HealthReel and became the first athlete to become a NASA technology partner. I asked Femi about that journey and the different elements that played a part in that success.

He said, "I have a bachelor's in psychology and an MBA from Hopkins, and I am a certified nutritionist and a former certified personal trainer. Every year prior to COVID-19, I tried to immerse myself in some learning environment to acquire another credential or certification...the last one I did was so valuable. I went to Harvard, to their Harvard extension school in Cambridge. I did a one-week program and received my advanced negotiation certification. I did that because I find myself talking to Apple, FitBit, Google, Microsoft. I'm checking off these educational boxes because they add value to the entrepreneurial closet that I have. I just pull out a different wardrobe that day for the task at hand."

Concept

Elite athletes are always adding to their tool box. These tools include knowledge on training and nutrition, new techniques, practice drills, rest and recovery regimes, and so forth. Elite athletes are constantly looking at their journey ahead and acquiring the tools that will help them outperform their competition.

Takeaway

Femi's post-NFL business career is a great example of preparation and planning for the journey ahead. To keep up with the changing business environment, leaders must always be acquiring new skills and knowledge. The best way to beat uncertainty is to be ready with the right tools at your disposal. Build your tool box—before you need it.

DEFY THE ODDS

Pat Woodcock
Strength Coach, Entrepreneur, and Creator of Elite Man Method
NFL/CFL Player, Grey Cup Champion

Pat grew up in a small town called Kanata, just outside Ottawa, Ontario. He played in the NFL for the New York Giants and Washington Football Team. During our chat, I was curious to know how Pat proved his critics wrong and made it to the NFL, despite being undersized as a receiver, as he put it, someone with "small hands."

Pat said, "I honestly think that many people have strong limiting beliefs. They don't believe they can lose that weight, they can get that job, they can play professional football. While it's true some of those things are not going to happen for everybody, people underestimate what their abilities actually are." In Pat's case, he went from being a big fish in a small pond to swimming with the sharks.

Concept

In sports, there are numerous stories of athletes who were never big enough, fast enough, or strong enough, who defied odds. From playing in the NFL to winning an Olympic medal, a big factor behind their success is their belief and will to win.

Takeaway

Making an impact at an organization and at an individual level starts with a positive mindset. In order to achieve the impossible, we need to first believe the impossible is true. It starts by eliminating any limiting beliefs. Commit, keep a positive mindset, and execute. As Pat said, "You'll be surprised at what you can achieve."

FOR TEAMS

DEFINE YOUR OLYMPICS

Anna Foli
Senior Director, FTI Consulting
Former Captain and Player, Ohio State and French National Volleyball Team

I was really excited to chat with Anna given her unique experience playing for both the French National and the Ohio State volleyball teams. I asked about her transition from elite volleyball to the corporate world, where she's held leadership roles for billion-dollar companies.

For Anna, the big change was going from competing for multiple championships a year, such as the European Championships or the Olympics, to an environment where there was no defined end. She said that in business, we also need to define our championship. It's important for each organization to "have clear, achievable goals, and, just like in sports, a few key plays to run and execute perfectly for their team to be successful." It's about making sure everybody in the organization understands their goal and is clear on how their role will contribute to the greater picture and success of the overall business.

Concept

Every year, every league across major sports crowns a champion. Some once a year (NHL), and some multiple times a year (professional tennis). Whether it's the Super Bowl, winning gold at the Olympics, a college championship, the FIFA World Cup, or any other championship, there is always a clear goal. Everyone knows what trophy they're competing for. All players work together to carry the ball to the end zone, and fans who have come to cheer for the team know exactly what they are about to experience.

Takeaway

Similarly, it's important to define the Olympics for your business. Why does your business exist in the first place, and what is that ultimate goal? Having a clear North Star, having well-defined objectives, and making sure each and every person on the team understands the significance of their role are key to building a high-performing team. After all, it's tough to make big plays if you're not sure what you're competing for and don't have a clear direction. Customers, just like fans, will grow their loyalty to a business that delivers consistent products or services and will keep coming back for the experience.

BUSINESS = TECHNOLOGY

Adam Zeitsiff
President and CEO, InteliVideo
Former Global CEO, Gold's Gym; Former CIO, Smoothie King

Adam was discussing his learnings as an entrepreneur before he ventured into the corporate world. Adam said, "It was me and my dog, my only responsibility in life. I said worse case, Mom and Dad will take me back. And we started a business in the video conferencing space...we grew it from nothing to a good-sized business. While I was there, I learned all about tech and software."

After his entrepreneurial journey, Adam led the technology function for many large brands including Smoothie King and Gold's Gym. Subsequently, he took on the role of CEO at Gold's Gym. Given it's rare to see a tech leader take on the reins of a business, I asked Adam what allowed him to make that transition. He credited the success to his experience as an entrepreneur. He said the five and a half years of working with the company that he had sold his business to were almost like business school for him.

Concept

Playing multiple roles and switching positions are common in sports. Players who can play different positions also tend to last the longest in the world of professional sports. It's very valuable for a coach to dress a player for a game who can step into different roles as needed. But it starts by being open to learning the fundamentals of a new position.

Takeaway

Today, technology and business are one, yet many leaders find it tough to connect the two. Technology is an enabler of business, and every business today must be built with a tech-first mindset. Therefore, leaders of tomorrow must combine the two to maximize impact in a digital-first world.

PEOPLE, NOT COMPANIES

Jessica Kuepfer
Director of Communications, Home Hardware Stores Limited
Endurance Athlete

An English literature major and French minor, Jessica was all set to become a teacher after graduation. Until she saw it in practice. "I realized I hated it...and for someone in their early twenties, it's like the end of the world." In hopes of a new career, Jessica heard about the chaos theory during a chat with her career advisor. It propelled Jessica to try new things, experiment, and explore her opportunities.

While working for a magazine and also as a personal trainer, Jessica ramped up her networking with mentors who she admired. During one of her coffee chats, she connected with her current boss. After the meeting, she knew for sure that she wanted to work for him. She took on a three-month contract position with the company. Jessica knew that once she had the opportunity, she would do everything in her power to overdeliver. A month and a half into that role, a full-time position opened up, and Jessica joined the company full time.

Jessica's boss at the time was a manager, and she joined as a coordinator. Today, he's a senior executive, and Jessica is the director of communications.

Concept

Teams that win have great chemistry. They may not have the best talent, but the commitment and promise the players and coaches make to each other are often more powerful than talent alone. Championship teams are made stronger through unbreakable bonds between teammates and coaches.

Takeaway

In business, people work for people. Organizations, companies, and cultures are all a reflection of their people. To be truly happy in disruptive times, surround yourself with the right people first, not just brand names that may look good on a résumé.

ENCOURAGE FAILURE

Mike Morreale
Commissioner, Canadian Elite Basketball League
Former CFL Receiver (twelve years) and Grey Cup Champion

In 2020, Mike and the new Canadian Elite Basketball League (CEBL) made history as the first sports league to return to play during the pandemic. I asked Mike what the biggest lesson was that he took from all of his years as a pro athlete that he had applied to standing up CEBL, amid a pandemic.

He said, "The first thing that pops to my mind is not having the fear of failure, and I learned that by failing. Sport was a teaching moment, repeatedly, day in and day out. It doesn't have to be the failure of a big drop in a touchdown pass, and, believe me, I've done that." As leaders, we need to push our teams outside the comfort zone and remove any fear of judgment, and that starts with the leadership taking and encouraging calculated risks. Otherwise, you risk being average.

Concept

Failure is everywhere in sports. Teams lose big games that they knew they should've won. A quarterback throws an interception. A top-ranked tennis player gets knocked out in the first round. But athletes also fail on a daily basis—failing to hit a personal best in the gym, missing practice shots, dropping a catch, or going off-side. It's through these failures that athletes build confidence to make big plays in big games.

Takeaway

Leaders and organizations must encourage failure and, more importantly, remove any negativity around it. A team that is afraid of making mistakes will never take big risks. And in a world full of uncertainty and disruption, playing it safe is ten times worse than failing along the way.

LEAVE EGOS AT THE DOOR

Brian Michael Cooper
Partner, Frost Brown Todd
Former President, Houston Roughnecks (XFL); Former President, Rio Grande Valley Vipers (NBA G League)

Brian Michael Cooper walked me through the three things that allowed him to succeed in a brand-new role as the president of RGV Vipers. First, he had a four-point plan that became his roadmap as the team president. Second, he focused on building trust with the leadership, partners, and fans.

Third, he said, "No job was too big or small. The great thing about leagues like the NBA G League is that there was no room for large egos. I always tell young people interested in working in the sports industry, 'Work in the minor leagues for a while.' Everyone is working together, and it's an ego-free zone." Brian would walk around the stadium during the games, and if he'd see garbage, he'd simply pick it up. He treated the stadium as if it was his own house, and he advised his staff to also treat the stadium as if it was their own house.

After four or five games, he saw that the fans started doing the same.

Concept

No one is too big or too small for any job. Building a strong team and gaining trust comes down to earning the respect of your teammates. Great athletes, coaches, presidents, trainers, and any other member of a sports organization know that earning respect comes from doing the best that you can to help the team win.

Takeaway

Leading in business against heavy headwinds and disruption requires all hands on deck. But in order for your team to conquer the biggest of challenges and make it through the ups and downs, it needs to buy into you as a leader. The team needs to have respect for the leader. And as seen in Brian's case, this comes from rolling up your sleeves, modeling the right behaviors, and doing whatever needs to be done, without ego or pride.

LOSE WITH RESPECT

Dr. Nick Bontis
President, Canada Soccer; Chair, Strategic Management, DeGroote School of Business; Keynote Speaker
Former University All-Star Soccer Player

I've known Dr. Nick Bontis since my first day at McMaster. He has always been a big supporter of the football team. As a former university all-star soccer student athlete, I asked Dr. Bontis what impact soccer had on his highly successful business and teaching career.

He shared a great memory from his university soccer days, where after a loss in the Ontario finals against University of Guelph, he went into their locker room. He said, "They were celebrating like crazy, and I walked into their locker room and shook the hand of every single individual and wished them luck." The head coach, twenty years later during his retirement, reached out to Dr. Bontis to tell him that he never forgot that moment.

Concept

Rivalry and competitiveness are what makes sports special. During a game, it's about going all out and leaving it all on the field. But once that whistle blows, the aggression, anger, resentment, and emotions are all left behind on the field. Off the field, athletes with class carry themselves with nothing but respect for each other.

Takeaway

Given the post-pandemic push for digitization and transformation, people and organizations are only going to increase their level of competitiveness. Winning leaders and businesses must be competitive but also respectful. You may experience a bad quarter, a negative review, a failed interview, or negative feedback. Those who move forward with humility and respect, despite losing the race, will be the ones who win the marathon.

ALWAYS GET UP, NEVER GIVE UP

James Yurichuk
CEO, Wuxly Outerwear
Former CFL Linebacker and Grey Cup Champion, Fourth Overall Draft Pick

James Yurichuk is a Brampton native and someone I looked up to during my high school football years. While playing in the CFL, he founded Wuxly through a kick-starter campaign in 2015. Today, the company has grown to seven-figure revenues.

Wuxly was all set to have one of the biggest years in 2020 as an animal-friendly luxury outerwear start-up, but COVID-19 put a dent in those plans. Luxury outerwear sales were down in 2020 across the industry. During our conversation, James said, "It was scary."

But through consistent push and resilience, Wuxly was able to secure a large manufacturing contract with the Canadian government to help produce PPE during the pandemic. James said, "We generally wanted to help. When I saw there was a call for Canadian manufacturers...it was like wartime efforts for manufacturers to produce things (PPE) to protect Canadians."

Wuxly was able to produce over seven million gowns in under three months, adding new life to the outerwear business.

Concept

The only time you fail is when you quit. Sometimes a bad call from the referee, an injury, or a bad play can really take a turn for the worse. But great athletes and teams simply get up and get back on track. They get after it, again, and again, and again.

Takeaway

Given the rise in consumer demands, availability of technology and new tech-first entrants, the post-pandemic world will be full of change, disruption, chaos, and uncertainty. Competitive pressures will continue to rise. Leaders who continue scratching and clawing even during the darkest moments can take their teams and businesses to new heights. After all, you may be just one opportunity away from turning it all around.

EMOTIONAL DETACHMENT

Alexandra Orlando
Director of Marketing, Panam Sports
Rhythmic Gymnastics Olympian and Five-Time Canadian National Champion
Commonwealth Games Record Holder for Most Gold Medals Won at a Single Event, Three-Time Pan-American Games Gold Medalist

Arguably the best rhythmic gymnast that Canada has ever seen, Alexandra Orlando is an Olympian and Commonwealth Games record holder who now heads up marketing for Panam Sports. We were discussing how to drop an idea and pivot from something that hasn't been working.

Alex said, "Even if you've invested the time, money, effort... if it's not working, and you're not getting the result, it's OK! And it's accepting that it's OK, and being able to move on, restrategize, and execute upon that. It's difficult (because) when we invest a lot of time in something, we feel we need to continue investing that time."

Concept

Feedback is instantaneous in sports. Athletes are able to see results almost instantaneously. The competitiveness and speed in sports push athletes to change course if needed, regardless of the time and effort that went into a certain program or training. Great athletes are always focused on getting to the top, and not fixated on a certain way of doing things.

Takeaway

Business results take time, especially for companies undergoing massive transformations. It's important to recognize that it takes strength and courage to change direction. It's never a good idea to throw good money after bad, just because you made an initial investment. Changing direction and pivoting has a much higher ROI in the long run than holding on to things that don't work in the short run.

BUILD EACH OTHER UP

Quinton Porter
VP, North America, Pico – Get Personal
Former NFL and CFL Quarterback

I remember watching Quinton Porter play for the Hamilton Ti-Cats during my university years. I was really excited to hear about his journey after football. I asked Quinton how he handles someone who's not pulling his or her weight. Quinton said it is always about the team. If there was an ego problem or a skill set problem, "Together, as a team, we can bring him up or bring him down to earth...as long as the overall vision of the team is primary.

From a skills standpoint, if someone wasn't supposed to be on the field, it was about helping them build confidence. I used to pull guys aside and say, 'You're here because you belong here. Don't question it. Who cares what anyone else has said? You've got this game to prove yourself; prove it now. Let's go. What are you going to do, cry and worry? Let's go.' I would always try to build people up."

Concept

If one player misses his or her assignment, the entire team suffers. This is especially the case in team sports where you rely on each other to get the job done. Instead of finger-pointing, great teammates help bring each other up, especially when someone is having a bad game or doubts their abilities. Great teammates take accountability for the team's overall performance.

Takeaway

When people point the finger, they're not only failing to bring that teammate up, but they're also absolving themselves of their own responsibility. This behavior hurts the people involved, it hurts the company culture, and it hurts overall company performance. When someone isn't performing, the best leaders (and teammates) look at themselves first and how they could have done better. They own it. They make (and maybe voice) an effort to be better themselves while simultaneously lifting that other teammate up. This approach has a much better impact on the player who needs to be lifted up. Taking ownership and subsequently lifting others up always has the best outcome for the team. Build each other up.

PROVE THEM WRONG

Jeff Adamson
Cofounder, Neo Financial; Cofounder, SkipTheDishes
Five-Time Canadian National Wrestling Champion and Pan-Am Games Medalist

Jeff Adamson cofounded SkipTheDishes, arguably one of the most successful tech start-ups in Canada, acquired by Just Eat for $200 million in 2016. The early days, though, were tough, hard, and at times disheartening.

During our chat, Jeff shared that in the early years they entered a business "pitch" contest at the University of Saskatchewan for a $50,000 prize. It was money they really needed at the time. They had made the finals and went up against two start-ups that they were 100 percent certain they would beat. After a stellar final presentation, Jeff said that they were so sure that they "had it in the bag...(they) started ordering stuff from Amazon" while waiting for the results.

But when the results came in, they finished second, with a prize of just $5,000. The same day, Josh, the other cofounder, showed Jeff a press release that DoorDash (competitor) just raised $17 million. A few minutes after seeing the news, Jeff said, "We just need to prove them wrong."

Concept

The underdog mentality is a big weapon in the world of sports. Many athletes and teams who were told they are not good enough have defied odds, and at times defeated the best of the best. It all starts with the underdog mentality.

Takeaway

Jeff's story is an example of someone who applied the same mentality from his wrestling career to growing one of the biggest start-ups in Canada. You may come up short. Others may shoot down your ideas. And your product launches and sales pitches may fail. But none of it matters as long as you're willing to constantly improve and are driven to win. It doesn't matter what others think. Just prove them wrong.

BONUS RESOURCE

Grab a free copy of the P.R.O. Business Depth Chart Drill to Reducing Turnover Risk and Boosting Performance

This concise yet powerful PDF resource is **"part workbook, part video course"**. The best part? It can be consumed and implemented in one sitting – giving you clarity on how to **de-risk your organization** in minutes – not weeks or months.

You also get access to Tanvir's exclusive online community, and digital transformation and leadership resources directly to your inbox.

Scan QR code below or visit www.tanvirbhangoo.com/bonus

ABOUT THE AUTHOR

P.R.O. Business Mindset strategist, speaker, and author Tanvir Bhangoo helps global companies transform, adapt, and lead in a digital-first world – connecting people, business, and technology via the P.R.O. Business Mindset.

He's the CEO of TB Momentum, a digital and leadership consulting firm that works with multinational businesses and Fortune 500's to help them transform and adapt to an ever-changing world. He has hosted the successful 'Sports to Business' Podcast since its launch in 2020.

Today, Tanvir shows organizations how to stay focused, adaptable, and influential in a disruptive and fast-changing world, through keynote speaking, workshops, and consulting.

Realizing that the success behind global digital transformations and his accelerated career came from the same principles that brought him success on the football field, Tanvir decided to reverse engineer these learnings and share them with the world.

The result? The P.R.O. Business Mindset framework, a revolutionary methodology built on the belief that people and execution – not just technology – are key to digital transformation success.

As a former VP of Technology at Freshii and Director at RBI (Tim Hortons, Burger King, Popeyes), Tanvir has led industry giants in end-to-end digital transformations, orchestrated multinational launches, and is a member of Forbes Technology Council.

When he's not speaking, Tanvir enjoys mentoring young athletes and coaching local football camps. And you can catch him working out at 5 AM; how he keeps off the 80lbs he lost post football.

HARNESSING THE POWER OF THE P.R.O. BUSINESS MINDSET

P.R.O. BUSINESS MINDSET KEYNOTES AND WORKSHOPS

TAKE THE P.R.O. BUSINESS MINDSET
FURTHER – ADAPT, LEAD, WIN

Tanvir inspires organizations to adapt, lead, innovate, and transform in the face of disruption and chaos. Integrating insights from his experience as a business executive and college football national champion, he challenges the way businesses approach disruption, empowering them to thrive and win in a tech-first world.

Speaking Topics include P.R.O. Strategy, Digital Transformations, Team Performance, and Leading Through Failure.

Visit www.tanvirbhangoo.com

TB MOMENTUM: TRAINING AND CONSULTING PROGRAMS

BUILD THE PLAYBOOK, TRAIN YOUR TEAM, EXECUTE AMID DISRUPTION AND CHAOS

Through The P.R.O. Business Mindset Programs, TB Momentum works with leadership teams and organizations to help them adopt championship winning principles in business, maximizing organizational and team performance in the digital first world.

Workshops, consulting programs, and digital courses focused on strategy, digital transformations, and team performance.

visit – www.tanvirbhangoo.com/consulting
visit – www.tbmomentum.com

ACKNOWLEDGEMENTS

I would like to thank my parents, Balwant and Gurcharan, and my younger sisters Manvir and Jaslin for all their support throughout my childhood, football journey and beyond. Thank you mom for the endless cooking, washing all my football laundry, and being my stretch partner before game days. I want to thank my wife Preet Garcha, for the daily motivational pep talks, her patience, and for putting up with me.

I would like to thank coach Ptaszek for making me a part of the McMaster Marauder family. A special thanks to all the coaches, from Frank Gesztesi for recruiting me, Carm Genovese and Mark Verbeek for always pushing me, Greg Knox for showing me the power of the championship mindset, and Roger Dunbrack, Nathan Finlay, Steve Lidstone, and Andrew Yap for their support. And a big thank you to my football brothers for all the great memories, through the ups and downs.

I would like to thank Professor Peter Vilks and Dr. Nick Bontis for introducing me to the concept of management. I want to extend a sincere thanks to Stephanie Hardman for providing me the opportunity that kickstarted my tech career. To Kelly MacPherson who took me under her wing, for placing me in the right roles, and for trusting me before I was ever ready. And to Matthew Corrin for believing in my leadership and for supporting me in pursuing my dreams.

When I started this project, I knew very little about publishing a book – but I was fortunate to be surrounded by some great folks. My thanks go first to my wife Preet, for being my toughest critic, for her constructive feedback, and for her support in building the P.R.O. methodology framework.

I would like to thank Jeff Adamson, for a relevant, strong and purposeful foreword to this book, without which this book would be incomplete.

I was fortunate to have the help of Dylan Andrews, a trusted friend, digital expert, and editor – It made a world of difference during the final stages of the book. It was great to have the team at Elite Authors assist with the wonderful cover design and final rounds of editing. I would also like to acknowledge my amazing team for their help and support on the podcast and digital efforts: Jaslin Bhangoo, Tavlin Sekhon, and Neha Bokhari.

Lastly, I would like to thank all the interviewees for sharing their insights, lessons, and wisdom with me, and for their support in launching this book. Thank you!